From the Living Room to the Bedroom

The modern couple's guide to sexual abundance and lasting intimacy

Advance Acclaim for
From the Living Room to the Bedroom

"The Bercaws have clearly identified the essential components of a healthy, long-lasting sexual/marital relationship. This book is a must read for couples in all stages of relationship, as it provides an easily understandable road map to having a great relationship. Busting the myth that relationships work on autopilot, the book reinforces respect as the bedrock for a solid and exciting sexual relationship. Kudos to the Bercaws for their efforts!"

- **Alexandra Katehakis,** MFT, Certified Sex Therapist, Certified Sex Addiction Therapist; author of *"Erotic Intelligence"* Founder, *The Center for Healthy Sex (Beverly Hills, CA)*

"In today's culture of quick-fix guides and gimmicks, it's no wonder couples are continually disappointed when the latest trick or technique doesn't solve their problems in the Bedroom. Drs. Bill and Ginger Bercaw illuminate the connection to what's going on in the Living Room and, in their uniquely encouraging and heartfelt voice, show you how to build a strong foundation of emotional intimacy. Their practical, actionable guide for couples is never preachy, clinical or overwhelming. In fact, it feels like an honest, uninhibited yet comfortable conversation with close friends (friends who just so happen to be doctors and have the relationship-healing answers you've so desperately been seeking!) I recommend it to anyone who wants to achieve a loving partnership filled with true Sexual Abundance."

- **Paige Parker,** Founder of mega-site, *DatingWithout Drama.com*

"The Bercaws have done it again. This delightful and easy to understand guide helps couples reenergize their intimate relationship -- emotionally, sexually and erotically -- all within a context of joy and positive expectation. Their guided instructions (Planned Intimate Experiences) have a down to earth feel that helps couples to explore and experiment in areas where they want to increase connection in a way that is not threatening. I applaud them in developing an easy to practice, fun and exciting way to help couples reach their intimacy goals and rekindle their desires and communication. Thanks to both of you!"

- **Barbara Levinson,** Ph.D., RN, LMFT Founder of *Center for Healthy Sexuality* (Houston, TX)
  Certified Sex Therapist Diplomate
  Certified Sex Addiction Therapist

"When you fall in love you may be repeating dysfunctional relationship patterns that you learned growing up. No matter what your history, *From the Living Room to the Bedroom* provides a pathway to developing greater sexual intimacy beginning with specific skills to assist couples in developing a foundation of safety and trust through intentional dialog and mindfulness. When a couple can effectively learn to light up the circuits in the brain with heartfelt communication and empathy, there is a natural *CoupleFlow* towards greater eroticism and sexual fulfillment. Through a variety of practical *Planned Intimate Experiences* (PIE's), couples learn to use each other's attachment style to both diffuse frustration, communicate vulnerability and return to a vibrant and playful sex life."

- **Jan Beauregard,** Ph.D., CSAC, CSAT, Certified Imago Therapist, *Integrative Psychotherapy Institute* (Fairfax, VA)

"Using relatable stories, humor and a plan of action, the Bercaws give readers the benefit of their personal experience as busy parents who have worked to keep their relationship alive, AND as experienced psychologists who have helped countless couples achieve vital relationships. By weaving together a big-picture view of what makes relationships thrive and practical tools that hold readers' hands step by step, this approach builds communication, trust and intimacy, in all aspects of relating. *CoupleFlow* can transform relationships and make families stronger."

- **Tina Bryson**, PhD., Co-author, *The Whole Brain Child* and *No-Drama Discipline*

"It isn't every day that you find a book that speaks to where you are, where you want to be, and how to bridge the gap between. In "From the Living Room to the Bedroom" it's all right there -- the blueprint for the relationship you always meant to have. What are you waiting for?!"

- **Elaina McMillan,** CHt, Host of *Naked Talk Radio*

"Couples are under more stress than ever, and I see it every day in the condition of their skin. That being said, I can always tell when a person is happy in their relationship; the glow of the relationship is reflected in the glow of their skin. Happiness and satisfaction cannot be discounted in the quest for beauty, and this book is a great tool for achieving such."

- **Harold Lancer,** M.D., author of *"Younger"* Beverly Hills, CA

"The Bercaws have created a unique model called, *"CoupleFlow"* which helps couples have two conversations simultaneously; one for emotional intimacy and one for sexual intimacy. They take you step by step, gently guiding you on transforming your connection with your partner. Understanding that novelty and secure attachment are key to a relationship, this book uses exercises and practical suggestions to take your relationship to the next level!"

- **Joe Kort,** Ph.D., LMSW, Certified Sex and Relationship Therapist, author, *Is My Husband Gay, Straight, or Bi?* Founder of the *Center for Relationship and Sexual Health*

Author's Note:
Every story in this book is a compilation of true experiences, and
each has been edited for clarity. Names and other identifying
information have been changed to protect confidentiality. *This
book is not intended to serve as a substitute for professional
treatment.* Though the principles and action steps in this book are
sound and effective, some people might find it helpful to take
deeper issues about sexuality (including dysfunctions, trauma and
sexual, physical or emotional abuse) to a therapist who can provide
customized treatment. In that case, this book can be a valuable aid
in the therapeutic process.

Table of Contents

Foreword
by Robert Weiss

Having spent the better part of my professional life (over two decades) as a sexual addiction and intimacy disorder's specialist, it makes sense that Drs. Ginger and Bill Bercaw might ask me to contribute here as my clinical work has lead me to write several books and literally hundreds of articles and blogs on topics similar to those they have written about. That said, with so many years helping couples with dysfunctional relationships and the problems evoked by broken, scarred and fragile attachments, I find myself more interested now than ever in the development and maintenance of emotional and sexual health within our intimate relationships. Today it seems less useful to simply address a couple's "sexual problems" as separate or discrete entity from the relationship as a whole.

To offer one example here- it has become increasingly apparent to me that when a committed spouse sexually or romantically cheats on their partner, it's not the cheating itself or any specific sexual act that causes the deepest pain. Rather, it's the betrayal of trust (often evoked by years of manipulation and outright lying), that hurts a formerly trusting partner the most deeply. What it takes for an emotionally betrayed spouse to heal and trust again takes more than simple admissions of guilt, "I'm sorry's" and begging for forgiveness.

Much of what I have learned over years of treating unfaithful, broken relationships is truly mirrored in the most pertinent issues laid out so expertly in this book. And the predominant theme of couple's healing and growth is simply this: *Ongoing, healthy relationship intimacy, sexuality and commitment involve a dedicated focus on relationship trust, where both partners are in the constant practice of being emotionally vulnerable, honest and transparent.* And that without these pieces in place and in practice there can be no genuine intimacy or meaningful ongoing connection to those we profess to love.

In truth, *the need for vulnerable, open and honest communication is as necessary in unscarred relationships that never experience sexual infidelity as it is in those more troubled coupleships.* As Drs. Ginger and Bill Bercaw address so well in this book, you don't have to sexually cheat to *drift apart* in an intimate relationship. Modern life with all its requirements and distractions is practically organized to encourage a *drift away* from those we love, even when we don't mess up our relationships by things like lying and cheating. Never-ending work, the ongoing needs of children, financial and other stressors, maintaining a home, self-care and all sorts of other time, energy, and emotionally consuming activities sap vitality and meaning from our primary connections. And sadly, much like the way we gain unwanted pounds, this kind of emotional distancing from those we simply *expect to always be there for us,* occurs bit-by-bit, day-by-day, often without us even realizing it. Left unattended, it is all too easy today

> *The need for vulnerable, open and honest communication is as necessary in unscarred relationships that never experience sexual infidelity as it is in those more troubled coupleships.*

to forget about our own, and in particular, our primary partner's needs for time, affection, attention, and intimacy. On our busy days (and there seem to be more of those every month it seems), we may even come to resent this "neediness" both in ourselves and therefore also in those we love, falsely believing that other aspects of our lives are more important -- if not long term, at least in this or that particular moment.

Sadly and without clear warning, our focus on actively loving ourselves and our partners can slowly fade away in moments, then weeks or months, and sometimes years. And this is how one achieves a non-intimate partnership, one where a couple remains together (for the kids, cause we've always been together, because it's easier than breaking up), but are more like two strangers passing in the night than treasured, appreciated, connected partners in life.

Is it any wonder that divorce is so prevalent in our society? The simple truth is that when primary relationships lose their priority, they wither on the vine. It doesn't matter how much we love our partner, or how physically attracted to that person we are or were. When we dismiss the need to actively nurture our relationships we are quite likely to lose that relationship, or at least lose the parts of our intimate connections that nourish us the most fully.

This is where *From the Living Room to the Bedroom* truly sings. This book recognizes why modern couples, increasingly pulled apart by so many understandable distractions, can make their day-to-day a higher priority than the active practice of remaining in love, resulting in emotional and physical intimacy falling by the wayside.

> *Modern life, with all its requirements and distractions, is practically organized to encourage a drift away from those we love, even when we don't mess up our relationships by things like lying and cheating.*

To this very point, the insights and exercises presented herein are simple, straightforward, and require relatively little time to implement, but they make such a difference! In fact, the suggestions and direction described in these pages are actually designed to be shoehorned into even the busiest of life/parent/work schedules (15 to 30 minutes, 1 to 3 times per week). Even better, these shared experiences typically return more positive energy when accomplished than the time and focus it takes to carry them out. So by following some of the techniques and direction in this book, in addition to recharging a relationship, couples can also literally help recharge their individual lives. And in our self-care deprived world, that's quite a little bonus! In fact, I fully expect that those who read, embrace and utilize the material presented herein will find themselves actually looking forward to these powerful and regenerative exercises as they encourage not only romantic reconnection, but also to remind each of us we it takes to remain heart-healthy and meaningfully connected.

Robert Weiss LCSW, CSAT-S
Author and Intimacy Disorder's Expert
RobertWeissMSW.com
Friday, February 14, 2014

Robert Weiss LCSW, CSAT-S is Senior Vice President of Clinical Development with Elements Behavioral Health. A licensed UCLA MSW graduate and personal trainee of Dr. Patrick Carnes, he founded The Sexual Recovery Institute in Los Angeles in 1995. He is author of *Cruise Control: Understanding Sex Addiction in Gay Men* and *Sex Addiction 101: A Basic Guide to Healing from Sex, Porn, and Love Addiction*, and co-author with Dr. Jennifer Schneider of both *Untangling the Web: Sex, Porn, and Fantasy Obsession in the Internet Age* and the newly released, *Closer Together, Further Apart: The Effect of Technology and the Internet on Parenting, Work, and Relationships.* He has developed clinical programs for The Ranch in Nunnelly, Tennessee, Promises Treatment Centers in Malibu, and the aforementioned Sexual Recovery Institute in Los Angeles. He has also provided clinical multi-addiction training and behavioral health program development for the US military and numerous other treatment centers throughout the United States, Europe, and Asia.

Preface

Dear Readers,

We might never have met you personally, but we probably know some things about you. We know your time is at an all-time premium and you are constantly choosing which priorities to defer until tomorrow. Your relationship is one of those priorities, but it is often the easiest to postpone. We know how little time you actually have together compared with how much time you'd like together. We know how tired you both become during the week, and how heavily scheduled your weekends are. We know that your typical weeknight conversation is often rushed and limited to the next day's schedule or children's needs -- and even those limited conversations can feel incomplete. We know you sometimes wonder if your partner really sees you, is really with you in your day to day life: *"Does he know how many things I've been juggling?" "Does she know how hard I've been pushing at work?"* We know the distance that can creep into your relationship when this wondering turns into serious doubt and your conflicts seem to stack up. If this distance reaches a tipping point, it can even seem as if you are living with an adversary who is working against you rather than with a partner.

With so little time and energy, it's easy for sex to fall off of the radar screen. Then, when you do have sex, it can seem almost obligatory, as if it's something you *should* be doing -- especially if it's been a while since the last time. It will never be mistaken for the passionate, eagerly anticipated sexual times that were so free and easy during earlier days together. So yes, we know how deeply you want your relationship to work, in the Living Room and the Bedroom, and how frustrating it can be when you realize it isn't working as well as it could.

However, we also know that sometimes you have a wonderful experience that reminds you why you got together in the first place: A good laugh about something only the two of you would really appreciate, an instance of really being there for each other, or a great time in bed. But these can seem almost random, with no clear path for channeling those feelings consistently. We know the fantasy -- "Once we just get past... [*insert looming event/project here*] we'll get back to normal; we'll get back to each other." We also know how elusive those anticipated turning points can be.

How do we know all this about you? Because we *are* you: A couple of crazy-busy, hard-working, well-intentioned but imperfect people trying to make their relationship work amid consistently challenging conditions. As Clinical Psychologists and Certified Sex Therapists, we've spent thousands of therapy hours helping others find relationship satisfaction, yet we do not get a free pass in our own marriage. Look at this list of potential relationship problems:

- Communication Obstacles
- Conflict Resolution
- Division of Household Labor
- Sexual Issues/Conflicts
- Work-Family Balance
- Financial Decisions/Budgeting
- Housing (location, affordability)
- Extended Family
- Childcare Decisions
- Family Health Issues

We know firsthand what it's like to have challenges in each of these areas. The natural flow of life just continues bringing them to us in a steady stream and we keep trying to keep up. And like you, we know all too well how easy it is to get swept away by the strong currents of the natural flow of life. Thankfully, we have also come to learn an even more powerful force: The power of a renewed commitment to make our relationship as strong as possible by *establishing the flow in our relationship that serves us best.* Our program, called ***CoupleFlow,***™ shows couples like us and like you how to harness that renewed power so your relationship can rise above the challenges presented by whatever conditions are swirling around you.

*****

Have you ever heard an athlete interviewed after a particularly brilliant performance? Many times they will refer to being in "the zone" or in "the flow" of the game. These are different ways of referring to the same concept. The following quote elaborates on these highly desired athletic experiences:

*"Athletes who are continually seeking to extend their limits and who have the necessary commitment to keep developing their skills to keep pace with ever-increasing challenges experience a tremendous sense of accomplishment from continuing to move their achievements to higher levels. Such athletes also experience the exhilaration of **flow** in what they are doing."*

-Susan A. Jackson and Mihaly Csikszentmihalyi, *Flow in Sports* (Human Kinetics, 1999).

Flow is a state of mind where everything just seems right. Fortunately, it's not exclusive to athletes or performers. It's entirely possible to create positive flow in just about any experience. This includes the experience of being in a relationship. Let's look at the above quote again, this time substituting the word "couples" for "athletes:"

*"**Couples** who are continually seeking to extend their limits and who have the necessary commitment to keep developing their skills to keep pace with ever-increasing challenges experience a tremendous sense of accomplishment from continuing to move their achievements to higher levels. Such **couples** also experience the exhilaration of flow in what they are doing."*

Notice the key phrases running through this description of flow: *"continually seeking to extend their limits"* and *"commitment to keep developing their skills."* Clearly, flow is not an accidental occurrence but the end result of dedicated and consistent practice while working toward an ambitious goal. This is the essence of the *CoupleFlow* model -- a sustainable exchange of positive relational energy between romantic partners that results from very intentional commitment to relationship prioritization.

> *This is the essence of the **CoupleFlow** model -- a sustainable exchange of positive relational energy between romantic partners that results from very intentional commitment...*

When you experience *CoupleFlow*, you'll enjoy the benefit of an energizing circulation between two separate but interconnected realms of your relationship: your emotional intimacy (Living Room) and your sexual intimacy (Bedroom). As you generate positive energy in each room, and this energy flows back and forth between the rooms, you will undoubtedly notice a powerful connection that keeps growing stronger.

It's likely that you already know a thing or two about *CoupleFlow*, having experienced a version of it earlier in your relationship together. If you think back to the easy days when you first fell in love, you probably recall a LOT of positive energy. You were just beginning to trust that your partner was, in fact, a partner. In the

Living Room, you couldn't wait to share all of your day's events and to be there for each other. In the Bedroom, you were

> *CoupleFlow reconnects you with the sources of those early romance feelings.*

powerfully drawn to each other, and couldn't wait to connect physically. These were the days of "can't get enough of your love." As a couple, you were *in the zone.* The goal of the *CoupleFlow* program is not to replicate the swept away feelings of early romance -- that would not be realistic. Instead, *CoupleFlow* reconnects you with the sources of those feelings: partnership, trust, respect, kindness, genuine interest, vulnerability, quality time and FUN. These sources are just as key today as they were then in maximizing the shared, positive experiences that keep you coming back for more and promote resilience during challenging times.

And here is what we know from our own less than perfect attempts to manage life's challenges: *If you just go with the flow, it will eventually lead you away from each other.* If you lack a plan, you are likely to have a less than adequate frequency of shared, positive experiences, and you will merely be *reacting* to problems as they surface. At a minimum, your reactivity and/or distancing will

> *If you just go with the flow, it will eventually lead you away from each other.*

create a slow, sometimes imperceptible drift between the two of you called Couple Drift™. This is the polar opposite of the intentional, relationship-focused characteristics of *CoupleFlow*.

We are so grateful for the relationship we have now, especially because we know how hard we've worked to get here. It is a far from perfect one, yet there is a night and day difference between the relationship we have now and the one we started with. Before we committed to change the way we *naturally* related with each other, we experienced the same predictable struggles that any couple would. We did not yet have the critical skill set necessary to change the flow in our relationship to one that consistently generated positive energy, and one that allowed us to efficiently recover from hurts and frustrations.

Our professional careers have focused on helping couples to recover from everyone's worst case scenario, sexual betrayal. In 2005, we developed *Sexual Reintegration Therapy*, a new treatment modality for these couples. We were struck by how even the most severely damaged couples all started out rather blissfully. They were genuinely excited to be together and tremendously looked forward to living happily ever after. But as time went on, life became more demanding and they began to drift apart, so far apart that the relationship plummeted into crisis.

We were also amazed at how dramatically these couples could transform the ways they related with each other once they began using the specific techniques of *Sexual Reintegration Therapy*. Following this structured program allowed them to develop and practice the skills necessary for greater intimacy and joy in their relationship than they ever dreamed possible. This transformation took them safely outside the natural flow that had taken them so far off course. They created a new relationship with each other grounded in equality, trust and respect. They set up systems to support the cornerstones of their new relationship strengths. They kept doing what was working and remained vigilant against drifting back into old patterns that did not serve them well. These new ways of relating kept their Living Room and Bedroom doors propped open, allowing their genuine love and care to flow through. Their dynamic changed from one that naturally created distance to one that intentionally created intimacy.

But at the same time that we were helping other couples experience breakthroughs, we realized that WE had to do a better job of practicing what we were teaching. We enlisted a professional to help us with our own relationship struggles and to cultivate the relationship skill set we knew we needed. This powerful therapeutic journey allowed us to experience firsthand that *great relationships don't just happen* as most of us typically assume to be true in the honeymoon phase of our relationships. On the contrary, great relationships are created and nurtured. The abundance that we have welcomed into our relationship is the result of a dedicated process of learning and practicing specific skills. It was the result of practicing our program, *CoupleFlow*.

*****

We know that you don't need another relationship self-help book, full of recycled ideas that may sound good but that often leave you wondering, "OK, *now what?*" That's why we wrote a book that we would read. Our book would need to be highly usable, and combine professional expertise with our personal experience of what has been most effective in our own, very real, relationship. It would also need to be efficient, able to fit within our busy lives while making our time together more valuable.

That's why we came up with the *CoupleFlow* model. At its core is the understanding that *you are constantly influencing the flow of relational energy between you and your partner.* This is why our program emphasizes building your relationship with your partner not just day by day, but moment by moment. This approach will allow you to enjoy a powerful flow of energy that consistently moves you toward each other in the Living Room and Bedroom. While *CoupleFlow* is designed to improve your sex life, it does not compartmentalize the Bedroom because we know that focusing solely on sexual satisfaction misses the all-important context in which any sexual experience occurs. That context is the relationship at large, especially the ever-changing conditions related to emotional intimacy. So as you are actively nurturing your emotional intimacy in the Living Room of your relationship, you are simultaneously rolling out the welcome mat for sexual intimacy in the Bedroom (what we call Sexual Abundance).

We know that *CoupleFlow* works, not only because it has worked for our clients, but because it has worked for <u>us</u>. There's nothing magic about it, just a very efficient, proven plan for re-prioritizing your relationship in ways that make a very noticeable difference. We are confident that you will find your efforts to be entirely worthwhile because we know the satisfaction that results from following that plan. Thank you for trusting us to be your guides.

Warm regards,

Bill and Ginger

Part ONE

How Does CoupleFlow Work?

"If our relationship, including our sex life, continued *exactly* as it is now, I would be happy for the rest of my life!"

When was the last time you had this thought? If it was recently, congratulations- you are part of a highly desirable minority! If it's been a while (or never), then you might be looking to make some changes. You might have tried to spice things up one way or another, perhaps even with some short-term success. Or perhaps you resigned yourself to the way things are, having tired of many attempts to find ways around impasses. Here's a quick way to see where you are at: Rate the following aspects of your Bedroom according to the scale below it:

_____ Frequency of Bedroom activities

_____ Initiation (who approaches whom)

_____ Sexual satisfaction   (arousal/orgasm/fun)

_____ Variety (activities/settings /positions)

_____ Sexual communication

1 = This is a significant concern.

2 = A lot of room for improvement

3 = It's OK, but could be even better.

4 = I feel good about this part of our sex life.

5 = I wouldn't change a thing!

Whether this quick assessment tells you that your Bedroom could use a minor tune up (total score in the 15-25 range) or is in need of significant modifications (1-14), an improved sexual landscape is within reach. *CoupleFlow* has helped hundreds of couples make lasting improvements in their sexual intimacy.

However, if you are looking for a gimmicky, try-a-new-position-that-requires-Olympic-gymnast-flexibility approach, this probably isn't the model for you. On the other hand, if the idea of deeply satisfying sexual intimacy integrated within a solid core of emotional intimacy sounds appealing, then you are definitely in the right place. The formula we utilize is simple and straightforward: *When erotic experiences are paired with deep emotional connection, the result is what we call "**Sexual Abundance**™."* In other words, a warm connection in the Living Room makes for a *very* warm connection in the Bedroom (or *whatever* room you happen to enjoy your Bedroom activities!) For something that sounds so basic, the typical arc of a long-term relationship presents inherent challenges to feeling consistently connected in your partnership. When couples come to us for help, we almost always see a history of red flags. Even when there has been an obvious traumatic event (e.g., betrayal) the relationship usually had some noticeable flaws long before the event came to light. To illustrate, here is a typical sequence of events:

1. ***Honeymoon Phase -- Newlyweds!*[1]**
   We are perfect together! We appreciate each other, we complement each other and we can't get enough of each other. Our sex is great, communication is great, and our relationship is great. Sunny skies ahead!

---

[1] For some couples, the honeymoon does not go well and it foreshadows challenges the couple will face.

2. ***Honeymoon fades (within 6-18 months)***
   The shine may not be as blinding, but we love each
   other despite getting on each other's nerves
   sometimes. We aren't having quite as much sex, but
   hey, we couldn't keep up that pace up forever! We
   don't talk quite as much but it's probably just because
   of all the other things we have going on.

3. ***Parenthood***
   Our priority is the children. Our sex life has clearly
   been pushed to the back burner. We are both so tired
   from work, our sweet little ones, and all of our other
   commitments. When we do have sex, it *is* still fun
   (by the way, when *was* the last time we had sex?)
   When we talk it's usually brief and often interrupted.
   Misunderstandings are becoming more of the norm.
   We still love each other and value our family, but is
   this really how it's always going to be? This is not
   exactly what I pictured when we said our vows.

4. ***False Advertising***
   OK, this is NOT what I signed up for! I am not being
   appreciated, my needs are not being considered, and
   I'm not being treated respectfully. We are not
   making time for each other. We argue more than we
   talk, our sex life is dull, and just who *is* this person
   I'm in a relationship with?

5. ***Call in the Paramedics!***
   I've been unappreciated for so long that I'm going to
   look out for number one from now on. Two can play
   this game. I don't even WANT to talk about it
   because I know it won't make any difference. It's
   becoming clear that I made a mistake by getting
   involved with this person.

It can take many years to reach the painful depths of #5, and this is the stage that funds divorce lawyers' vacation homes. But many couples never bottom out in such obvious ways. *Just as common are the relationships that exist in a perpetual state of tolerable dissatisfaction or indifference.* They've been worn down and have accepted that "This is just how it's going to be."

> *These are the couples that celebrate anniversary after anniversary without addressing the distance they've been living with.*

They choose to endure for many reasons (for their children, for fear that they would be shunned by their families, that they would suffer financially, etc.), settling for a level of disconnection that they never imagined they would settle for. Some are not even all that aware that they are settling for less than what their relationship could be. But even if you are generally happy with your relationship, there is no shame in acknowledging that it could benefit from some extra attention. Just like physical exercise, you know you can't coast and expect to maintain fitness. You can be generally content with your body as it is now and still seek new ways to keep it healthy and strong.

But if your relationship *is* struggling and you can identify with #3, #4, or #5, consider how little you actually knew about how to nurture and care for a romantic partnership when you first committed to each other. From this standpoint, it would be more surprising if you consistently experienced relationship satisfaction than if you did not. Creating and maintaining a healthy relationship is like any other project where the outcomes can vary - - there is a *basic skill set* that is required for relationship success. What type of training did you have in developing a mutually satisfying romantic relationship? Well, what actually passed for training was everything you absorbed from your parents' marriage, supplemented by Hollywood and pop culture in general (think

Cosmo, Men's Health, talk radio, *The Bachelor*, soap operas, romance novels, and the *Internet*).

When you think about it some more, what other project or responsibility have you taken on that required such a critical skill set that you possessed so little of? And in what other circumstance would you ever get into a situation with someone you were depending on who *also* possessed a fundamental lack of training in a critical area? Would you get on an airplane with a pilot who had no formal training? How about if s/he had seen a lot of cockpit scenes in movies and television? Still -- NO! However, that's exactly what most of us do when entering into romantic relationships. We take off fast and hope for the best. Is it any surprise that it can be such a bumpy ride that sometimes results in a crash? Is it any surprise that even when you find yourselves in a good groove that the good times can come to a screeching halt?

It's one thing for us to put this universal challenge in metaphorical perspective and quite another to find a solution -- and that's exactly what this book does. Our first book, *The Couple's Guide to Intimacy,* was written

> *Intimacy is the heart and soul of CoupleFlow.*

for couples who had been clearly struggling (#4 and #5 territory for sure!). It gave them a path out of the dark abyss of secrecy, betrayal and avoidance and into the light of true intimacy. We soon realized that our treatment model for these couples was not just for people on one extreme end of the intimacy continuum, but one that could work for *anyone* in a long-term, committed relationship. Why? Because *all couples* seek to move into that light, regardless of their starting positions. All successful relationships are built on mutual appreciation of the fundamental meaning of intimacy -- the process of allowing yourselves to be *truly known by each other.* Intimacy is the heart and soul of

CoupleFlow, as it creates an ever-increasing, favorable atmosphere for bonding in the Living Room and Bedroom.

There is an unlimited potential for intimacy in your relationship, but your movement into that potential is dependent on two variables: (a) your ability to cultivate a higher level of relationship focus (and tolerating the accompanying vulnerability), and (b) knowing specifically *what* to focus on. The most efficient way to raise focus and to direct it toward areas that will have the biggest impact is by using a plan. This book provides that plan so the improvement process can be as straightforward as possible. It is not dependent on perfect execution, but on consistency. Some couples choose to do every exercise in the program, some do most exercises, and others pick and choose. However you use our *CoupleFlow* program, it all begins with shining a spotlight on the two most important rooms in your relationship house: your Living Room and your Bedroom. With this plan, the passionately connected relationship you had in mind back when you committed to each other is closer to your reach than ever before.

More FLOW

According to Mihaly Csikszentmihalyi, individuals have to *actively do something* to enter a flow state. That is why CoupleFlow emphasizes targeted action steps. Csikszentmihalyi's flow theory proposes three conditions necessary to achieve a flow state, each of which is incorporated in CoupleFlow's design principles:

1. You must be involved in an activity with a clear set of goals and progress. This adds direction and structure to the task.
2. The task must have clear and immediate feedback. This helps you negotiate shifting wants and needs, allowing you to adjust your actions to maintain the flow state.
3. You must have a good balance between your *perceived* challenges of the task and your own *perceived* skills. You must have confidence in your ability to navigate successfully and consistently with the task at hand.[1]

WORLDS APART: *COUPLEFLOW* VS. COUPLEDRIFT

There are some things that just don't go together. Oil and water. Cats and dogs. Orange juice and toothpaste. Add *CoupleFlow* and *CoupleDrift* to the list. Whereas *CoupleFlow* represents the positive stream of relational energy that enables Sexual Abundance, *CoupleDrift* is the term we use to describe the negative stream of relational energy that creates distance between partners. It is characterized by reacting instinctively to situations with your partner and being swept away from one negative interpretation and response to the next. It lacks self-discipline and drives a wedge between partners, creating a rising tide of negative assumptions, resentment and sexual dissatisfaction that gathers momentum as it continues.

In the arc of a typical relationship, your focus on each other is in increasingly greater competition with other areas of focus (children, careers, etc.). Thus, *CoupleDrift* is often quite subtle, with layers of distance

> *CoupleDrift is often quite subtle, with layers of distance slowly accumulating through the years.*

slowly accumulating until it becomes more obvious that there may be a problem. The Living Room and the Bedroom begin working against each other in *CoupleDrift*, so that instead of Sexual Abundance, each partner finds an abundance of evidence to support negative beliefs about each other and their relationship (e.g., "He doesn't care about me." "She's always mad about something." "There's no way to keep him happy." "I'll never be good enough for her.").

Sharing a life together presents a steady stream of potential challenges that can accelerate the cycle of *CoupleDrift*. These challenges cover a wide spectrum and include:

- Job stress/fear of job loss/actual job loss
- Business travel
- Career decisions
- Illness: personal, child, parent/in-law
- Financial concerns
- Family meals
- Holidays/birthdays
- Sibling relationships
- In-law relationships
- Household division of labor
- Fatigue
- Sexual desire differences
- Sexual dysfunction, addiction, sexual betrayal
- Volunteer commitments
- Leisure time preferences
- Long-term planning

All couples drop down into some degree of *CoupleDrift* at least once in a while. But in its advanced stage, it becomes a way of life, reinforcing recurring arguments and leading you to blame each other when things go wrong. It then becomes easy to find believe that your partner isn't really *with* you. In *CoupleDrift*, there may be stretches without conflict, but it mainly may be due to your avoiding each other. *CoupleDrift* can lead you to deep relationship dissatisfaction, where conflicts multiply until emotional exhaustion is the norm and it's hard to remember the last time you felt joy in your relationship. So as you look at the figures on the following pages, notice the contrasts between identical places on each circular chart. And if you identify some aspects of *CoupleDrift* that are present in your relationship, don't despair. That recognition could be just the spark you've needed to shift from drifting apart to flowing together.

Figure 1:

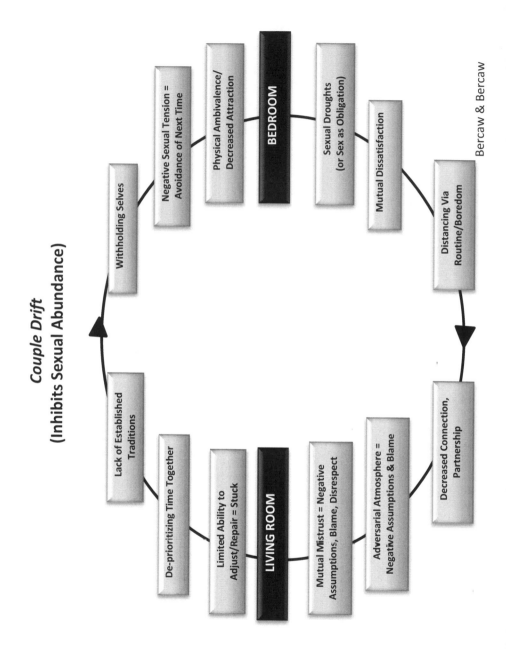

Couple Drift
(Inhibits Sexual Abundance)

BEDROOM

Negative Sexual Tension = Avoidance of Next Time

Physical Ambivalence/ Decreased Attraction

Sexual Droughts (or Sex as Obligation)

Mutual Dissatisfaction

Withholding Selves

Distancing Via Routine/Boredom

Lack of Established Traditions

Decreased Connection, Partnership

De-prioritizing Time Together

Adversarial Atmosphere = Negative Assumptions & Blame

Limited Ability to Adjust/Repair = Stuck

Mutual Mistrust = Negative Assumptions, Blame, Disrespect

LIVING ROOM

Bercaw & Bercaw

Figure 2:

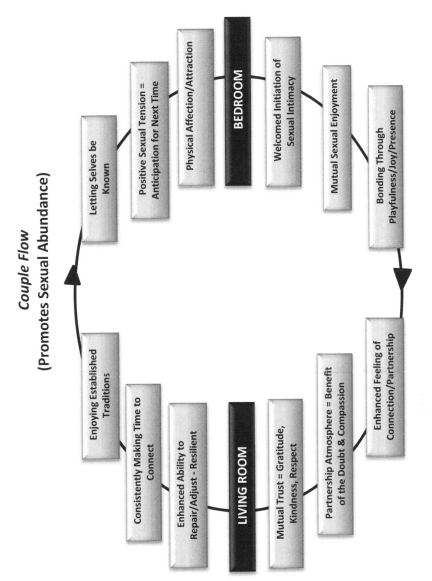

Couple Flow
(Promotes Sexual Abundance)

- Letting Selves be Known
- Positive Sexual Tension = Anticipation for Next Time
- Physical Affection/Attraction
- **BEDROOM**
- Welcomed Initiation of Sexual Intimacy
- Mutual Sexual Enjoyment
- Bonding Through Playfulness/Joy/Presence
- Enhanced Feeling of Connection/Partnership
- Partnership Atmosphere = Benefit of the Doubt & Compassion
- Mutual Trust = Gratitude, Kindness, Respect
- **LIVING ROOM**
- Enhanced Ability to Repair/Adjust - Resilient
- Consistently Making Time to Connect
- Enjoying Established Traditions

Characteristics of CoupleFlow:	Characteristics of CoupleDrift:
*Consciously chosen	*Unconscious autopilot mode
*Intentionally relational	*Unintentionally non-relational
*Receptive + Proactive = Vulnerable	*Distant + Reactive = Invulnerable
*Grateful for "WE"	*You vs. Me
*Joy / love/ gratitude based	*Fear / pain/ shame based
*Produces bonding hormones (oxytocin)	*Produces stress hormones (cortisol)
*Neurobiologically co-regulating	*Neurobiologically co-escalating

THE CIRCULATION MODEL OF *COUPLEFLOW*

Sometimes a struggling couple will walk into our office and the rhetorical question on their minds is, "How much *worse* can things get?" As understandable as that question may be, *CoupleFlow* poses a question from the completely opposite perspective: **"How GOOD can things get?"** The answer depends entirely on the quality of the circulation between your Living Room and the Bedroom. When there is proper circulation, each room benefits from the positively charged atmosphere in the other room, creating a balanced, self-renewing, positively charged feedback loop. *CoupleFlow* promotes each partner in taking charge of their own contributions to this relational energy, with no upper limit on just how powerfully positive your *CoupleFlow* can become.

The idea that you can have good flow in one room without the other is simply not realistic. However, gender stereotypes have traditionally painted a picture where men enjoy sex without needing much of an emotional connection, while women prioritize emotional connection and can do without sex. More recently, it has been viewed as progress in some circles that women can enjoy casual, detached sex as much as men. The fact is, everyone is entitled to equal enjoyment of sexual pleasure, and everyone wants to enjoy a deeply connecting emotional intimacy. *CoupleFlow* is designed to promote this type of well-balanced partnership, with erotic experiences being a very important aspect of the partnership, but not the focal point. So the essence of *CoupleFlow* is this: *When you consistently integrate emotional connection with erotic experiences, the Living Room and Bedroom will energize each other and create a freely flowing, deepening foundation of secure, renewable, limitless intimacy.*

For example, when you are enjoying sexual pleasure, the Bedroom door is not sealed shut. Rather, the positive energy from the Living Room continues to circulate inside the Bedroom while the Bedroom energy finds its way to the Living Room. Have you noticed how much more enjoyable sex is when you are really feeling closely connected to your partner? The passion flows naturally, as does the laughter, fun and excitement. Have you also noticed how much closer you feel when you're in a good groove sexually? It feels warm, comfortable and even flirty around each other[2].

---

[2] Some people experience anxiety when they feel their relationship becoming more intimate, and they respond by creating distance in one way or another to relieve the discomfort. If this pattern sounds familiar to you, or if you recognize it in your partner, you would be wise to consult with a licensed therapist who can help you with this complicated but treatable dynamic. If you would like to work with us but are not in the Los Angeles area, contact us to see if we may be able to help via phone or videoconferencing.

Every exercise in the *CoupleFlow* program has been designed with the purpose of helping

> *Have you noticed how much more enjoyable sex is when you are feeling closely connected to your partner?*

you to create the flow of emotional and sexual energy that works best for your relationship. While *CoupleFlow* emphasizes balance between your Living Room and Bedroom, it certainly does not place a ceiling on sexual pleasure. This will become more obvious as you progress through many of the exercises in this book, when you will be elevating your Bedroom connection and building toward Sexual Abundance.

WHAT *IS* SEXUAL ABUNDANCE?

Sidney stared at herself in the mirror, not loving what she saw. Crow's feet were making an earlier appearance than she anticipated, the circles under her eyes were becoming darker, and her skin looked as tired as she felt. As she moved her gaze downward, she was reminded that her body had not bounced back from her last pregnancy as she had hoped and she really couldn't blame her husband, Aaron, for not being more sexually interested in her.

Truthfully, Sidney wasn't all that interested in sex with him lately either. When they did have sex, it was a largely unspoken routine conducted in darkness, a far cry from their early days of eager anticipation, innuendos and verbal foreplay. A few years ago, he suggested they watch some porn together and she agreed, thinking maybe this would provide the spark that they needed. She did find it arousing, but couldn't help thinking Aaron was more turned on by the video than by her. Did he really need that to enjoy sex with her? They were drifting sexually and otherwise, and had been for some time. She had tried many times to express this to Aaron, but always ran into a wall of defensiveness or his annoying attempts to fix everything in one neat little phrase (e.g., "Why don't you just wake up a little earlier so you can work out?"). Paying less and less attention to each other, the consistency of their date nights had been surpassed by the consistency of their conflicts. Their Bedroom was getting monotonous; their Living Room was growing cool and distant. Maybe she would try waking up a little earlier...

*****

The challenging and ever-shifting landscape that characterizes emotional closeness and passionate sexuality is challenging for many couples like Sidney and Aaron. This is true despite an endless stream of perspectives and products on the topic presented in books, magazines, seminars, talk-shows, and even infomercials. But passionate, healthy sexuality within *CoupleFlow* centers around something different, what we call *"Sexual Abundance."*

Abundance as a lifestyle approach is hard to beat, as it involves believing that you are deserving of good things, and trusting that you will have what you need and will be able to deal with life's challenges. It is a strength-based approach that is fueled by *vulnerability*[3], in which you are receptive to love, nurturance and requests from others. It is the opposite of scarcity, which is fear-based, reactive, and restrictive, with low vulnerability tolerance. Knowing that you have enough of what you want and need, and finding satisfaction even as you strive to improve breeds *gratitude*, a tremendous life force that reinforces your belief in living abundantly. So why shouldn't such a wonderful approach to life in general follow you into the Bedroom?

That is exactly what happens with *Sexual* Abundance. It is not to be mistaken with sexual excess, but instead is the natural result of

---

[3] For an outstanding resource on the relationship between vulnerability and abundant living, we highly recommend *"Daring Greatly,"* by **Brene Brown**.

your sexual intimacy being in alignment with your emotional connection. Living Room to Bedroom and Bedroom to Living Room, the intimate connection circulates, grows stronger over time and allows you the security of knowing you have something that is very, very good. It may vary with some ups and downs, but you know that the system you have in place will carry you through challenging stretches. You know your sex life is great as it is, and you trust that it always will be. Why? One reason is because sexual intimacy in committed relationships is fueled by emotional connection. In this way, the source of Sexual Abundance keeps giving as long as the relationship keeps getting nurtured. It is an ongoing and renewable experience grounded in trust, respect, equality, fun, vulnerability and, of course, pleasure.

WHY YOU *MUST* TALK ABOUT "IT"

While it's common to avoid discussing your sexual intimacy, there is a very simple reason why avoidance will not serve your long-term interests: *Your sexual intimacy is an essential source of bonding in your relationship.* Stopping short of giving it the full attention it deserves deprives you of the chance to maximize its bonding potential.

> *The new normal is defined by consistently enjoying erotic experiences with the one you love, admire, and trust more than any other...*

Less than clear communication also places a ceiling on your pleasure potential since the *best* way for your partner to know what you like is to tell and/or show your partner. It's common to not even realize how you've been settling for a less satisfying status quo simply by not talking (or not talking enough) about sex with your partner. Sometimes it seems that there is so much lost time to make up for, that it would require more energy than you've got. However, we have seen many couples decide to stop settling and to start creating a new way that is marked by deep connection on a sexual, emotional and spiritual level. When the new normal is defined by consistently enjoying erotic experiences with the one you love, admire, and trust more than any other, the idea of settling will be a distant memory.

NOT *JUST* SPICING THINGS UP...BUT YES, SPICING THINGS UP

It is entirely possible to achieve this shift, but first let's look at how *not* to move in that direction. Within the hyper-sexual culture that surrounds us, there is a classic case of "good-news, bad-news." The good news is that we live in an era with more material available on sexual satisfaction than ever. The bad news is *also* that we live in an era with more material on sexual satisfaction than ever. The available menus of techniques to increase sexual satisfaction are seemingly endless, found in thousands of websites and in checkout stand magazines everywhere. You can spend a lifetime picking from these menus, hoping that the next variation, trick or method was what's been missing. You might even find some of the items to be helpful because you reach a higher level of arousal or enjoy an increase in sexual frequency.

For couples in stable relationships where both partners are experiencing sexual satisfaction, picking items from these menus to spice things up can be a fine thing to try. Yet, it could be that you have tried many of the above options without any lasting improvements. The fact is that any new "hot sex" technique *on its own* is likely to yield only short-term gains, if any. Couples usually find themselves circling back to their familiar routines, interacting through well-worn patterns, often creating very subtle layers upon layers of distance (think Sidney and Aaron). To avoid this rut, or to improve an already decent sex life, you need to get beyond merely superficial boosts. You need to address your sex life from within in order to bolster the source of Sexual Abundance: *Intimacy*.

SEXUAL ABUNDANCE IS ALL ABOUT *INTIMACY*

Despite a cultural bias against hot, exciting, passionate, monogamous sex, we believe that the *best sex* you will ever know is experienced in true intimacy with your partner. Erotic experiences on their own (e.g., one-night stands) are a dime a dozen, and not terribly difficult to facilitate. But erotic experiences in the context of a fully present, deeply loving and closely connected intimate partnership are something very special. It truly is a privilege reserved for those fortunate enough to have a committed partner to experience life with.

One of the concepts we use to describe the process of having our needs, wants and preferences met in relationships is "interdependence." Ideally, you are not on an island, trying to do everything yourself. You are also not looking to do everything *with* your partner or have him/her do everything for you, including making you feel good about yourself (This idea of couple's enmeshment as Bedroom-killer was brilliantly presented in Esther Perel's instant classic, *"Mating in Captivity"*). The goal, of course, is to live somewhere in the middle. Therefore, an ongoing task for any couple is to discover how *an interdependent sexual intimacy can grow out of an interdependent emotional intimacy.* In the case of Sidney and Aaron, one area they will definitely need to address so they don't keep spinning their wheels in their Bedroom is the way they connect with each other in their Living Room. The following figure illustrates the continuum that exists around interdependence. [4]

---

[4] Adapted from Pia Mellody

Interdependence

Extreme ← → Extreme

Moderate

Too Dependent

Anti-Dependent

*No boundaries
*Too sensitive
*Everything is personal
*Over-invested in relationship
*Feels like a victim

***Flexible boundaries
*Equals in relationship
*Self-reliant but can ask for help
*Mutual respect
* Can negotiate aspects of relationship
*Clear and direct communication
*Appropriately shares reality
*Accepts spouse's differences/ limitations
*Does not change /rescue or manipulate spouse**

*Rigid boundaries
*Too insensitive
*Too detached
*Under-invested in relationship
*Feels like a bystander

SEXUAL ABUNDANCE COMPONENTS

Sexual Abundance involves three primary concepts (each occurring in an atmosphere characterized by fun, grace, gratitude and freedom)

> (a) Establishing mutual commitment
> (b) Embracing your self-worth
> (c) Communicating your sexual realities

ESTABLISHING MUTUAL COMMITMENT

Because healthy sexuality can be experienced in different contexts, we need to distinguish between sexuality in non-committed relationships and in monogamous relationships. Being sexual in non-committed relationships does not require much effort at all. For example, there are websites with millions of openly married subscribers looking to meet other married subscribers for everything from a "quickie" to an ongoing

> *"Desiring another person is perhaps the most risky endeavor of all. As soon as you want somebody - really want him - it is as though you have taken a surgical needle and sutured your happiness to the skin of that person, so that any separation will now cause a lacerating injury."*
> - Elizabeth Gilbert

sexual relationship, with no strings attached. Many people can have very pleasurable, high-intensity sex via casual hook ups, paying for sex, or during porn-fueled sex with themselves, only to struggle with low desire, arousal problems and other sexual dysfunctions in a committed relationship.

While it is certainly possibly to experience healthy sexuality in many contexts, what we call Sexual Abundance is reserved for two people who respect each other completely, honor and protect their exclusive relationship, and value their exclusive commitment to each other. Making a commitment to exclusivity (whether married or not) is not everyone's cup of tea, and doesn't need to be. The fact is that so much more is required of each person's capacity for intimacy in order to experience a rich, satisfying sex life in a monogamous, mutually committed relationship. It doesn't mean that one type of relationship is "good" (monogamous) while others are "bad" (non-committed). It simply means that when you sign up for mutual commitment, it comes with the challenge of playing ball -- in the Living Room and Bedroom -- with a single teammate whom you will be thrilled to play with at times, frustrated by at others, honoring your team at all times, regardless.

SELF-WORTH IS SO...SEXY?

When you possess a healthy sense of your inherent worth, you feel good about yourself from within. While it feels good to receive compliments, affirmation and positive feedback from your partner, you are not dependent on external reinforcement to feel good about yourself. This becomes especially important as it relates to your sexual relationship. Reinforcing a positive sexual self-image is a key element of *CoupleFlow* that leads to Sexual Abundance. For example, it is always within your power to embrace thoughts, feelings and experiences that support your sense of being worthy of a nurturing, loving sexual relationship. This includes everything from how you feel about your body and how you care for it to how you feel about giving and receiving sexual pleasure. If you identify deficits in areas such as these, *CoupleFlow* will help you take steps to address them.

Consider Sidney's typical automatic interpretations when she noticed Aaron's decreased sexual interest. She would tell herself that Aaron didn't love her, or that something was wrong with her for not knowing how to stay more sexually relevant and appealing to him. This is far beyond what would be normal disappointment , concern and even self-reflection. It would be helpful for her to understand that such negative, automatic interpretations are usually repetitions of deeply ingrained messages from childhood. They have a very detrimental effect on adult relationships and often lead to feeling stuck. The antidote is to identify the sources of such outdated, inaccurate messages and to replace them with a more reality-based, adult way of thinking.

For example, while understanding Sidney's disappointment and frustration, we would want her to understand that Aaron's sexuality is about *him*. (Ideally, Aaron would address his sexual feelings with the aid of a therapist). His behavior does *involve her*, and for that reason she is on solid ground to communicate how she is experiencing him and what she would like to be different (e.g.,, "Aaron, when you say I should wake up earlier to work out, I think you're trying to fix me so I'll be more attractive to you. I know you probably mean well, but I want you to know that I'm struggling with my body image, and that suggestion isn't helpful."). Notice how she can reveal her truth without being either too meek or too combative. Yet as she does this, it is critical that she knows that her self-worth has nothing to do with Aaron's response to her, let alone his sexual interest in her. Rather than depending on Aaron for a sense of security, and then becoming resentful when he "fails" to provide it, she can reinforce her own ability to make herself feel secure by reminding herself, "I don't like Aaron's indifference to me, but I am not going to chase his approval." This may also help Sidney feel more confident in asking Aaron to partner with her so they can both enjoy more connection in the Bedroom.

SHARING YOUR SEXUAL REALITIES

Communicating as clearly as possible about your sexual realities is essential for the experience of Sexual Abundance. This means you are consistently sharing your requests, thoughts and feelings as they relate to your sexuality (more on this later in this chapter). This includes your desires, wants, curiosities, comforts, concerns, limits and gratitude, each of which is subject to change and therefore calls for ongoing communication. To help jumpstart your communication, you will be taking a self-assessment in Chapter Three, the *Sexual Preferences Survey*. It will be a springboard for identifying your preferences for various sensual and sexual experiences and for talking openly about them. You'll also be learning the skill set required for safely communicating in Chapter One.

As valuable as it is to share your sexual realities with each other, we must stress how important it is to do so in a way that feels safe. The safest way to share anything with each other is by making good use of your personal boundary system. This involves a very deliberate approach to sharing your truth and to receiving your partner's truth. The foundation of this approach is respect: respect for yourself, by giving a voice to things that matter to you; and respect for your partner, by recognizing that s/he is entitled to his/her own reality, even when it differs from yours.

The use of boundaries raises your intimacy potential by allowing you to be vulnerable but in a moderate and controlled way. If you are like us, you will appreciate how your boundaries allow you to communicate honestly and directly -- like adults -- about what really matters to each of you, from the Living Room to the Bedroom. You'll be learning a tried and true method for communicating this way in Chapter One. By the way, if all of this seems a bit foreign to you, we encourage you to hang in there, and by the end of the next chapter you'll know exactly what we mean!

YOUR BRAIN ON *COUPLEFLOW*

When we talk about creating an optimal flow of energy between your Living Room and Bedroom, we are also talking about creating an optimal flow of energy *between your brains.* The psychological term for this is *"interpersonal integration."* [5] Thankfully, you don't have to be a neurobiology expert in order to appreciate when something very good is happening in your relationship. But it might enhance your experience of *CoupleFlow* to know that every time you direct your energy toward your partner, you are having a direct impact on each of your brains: sending affirming or flirtatious text messages, gazing deeply into each other's eyes, slowing down to savor a caress or to communicate more empathically, revealing some vulnerability. Each of these can facilitate deep resonance between your internal worlds and promote a secure attachment bond between you. And thanks to recent brain research, we know that consistently experiencing your partner in nurturing, safe and trusting ways actually changes the wiring in your brains.

So not only are these loving behaviors good in the moment, they strengthen the neural connections in your brain so that you are likely to have more and more moments like it. Most of the action is taking place in the right hemispheres of your brains. This is where non-verbal information, like an open posture or a compassionate facial expression, is perceived and given meaning (e.g., *"My partner is here for me and it is safe to share this with him/her."*) It is also in the right hemisphere where emotion is accessed, thereby allowing you to connect in ever-deepening ways with your partner.

---

[5] For more on this topic, we recommend Dr. Dan Siegel's book, *Mindsight: The New Science of Personal Transformation* (Bantam, 2010).

When your right hemispheres are resonating with each other, you feel an energized bonding that keeps you coming back for more. You feel safe with each other. You can respect your differences and give each other the benefit of the doubt. When you do argue, no one walks away feeling like a loser. You trust that your partner is with you -- not necessarily *perfectly* tuned into to you, as that's not realistic for anyone -- but *consistently* tuned in to you, mindful of and responsive to your preferences, your struggles, and your experience of things.

When this attunement is working in both directions, it leads to mutual feelings of empathy and compassion, and to shared positive experiences that strengthen the fabric of your relationship. During such moments of attunement in the Living Room and Bedroom, your brains are awash in bonding and pleasure neurochemicals like oxytocin, vasoporin and dopamine. When your brain develops a taste for these powerful hormones, it wants more. Who knew that being hormonal could be such a *good* thing?

On the flip side, when you experience a "miss" (misattunement, to be precise), which includes everything from name-calling to stonewalling to criticizing, your brain is affected in an opposite manner. It releases the stress hormone, cortisol. The limbic regions of the brain (e.g., amygdala and hippocampus), where painful emotional memories are stored from your earliest days, is susceptible to being triggered. In a flash, you do not feel like your partner is with you as an ally. In the absence of empathy and compassion, you look warily at each other. From this place, your brain is prone to slipping into an aggressive stage (fight), an avoidant state (flight) or a dissociated/"checked-out" state (freeze).

These primitive states severely limit your ability to relate in a respectful, adult manner with each other (as you will see in more detail with the contrast between the *"Children's Menu"* and the *"Adults' Menu"* in Chapter One). The communications and actions that arise from these primitive states put great strain on the fabric of your relationship. The result is a sense of drifting apart.

Clearly, there is a lot going on behind the scenes whether you are cultivating closeness or drifting apart. Every exercise you find in the *CoupleFlow* program is designed to bring each of your brains (especially the right hemispheres) closer together, consistently strengthening the relational connections in your brains and the felt connections between you. Now we will explore how those connections can be nurtured in the Bedroom.

WHAT'S OLD IS NEW AGAIN

CoupleFlow is designed to improve your sex life immediately and also to promote enduring sexual satisfaction. Conventional wisdom and popular culture seem to suggest that the best way to increase sexual

> *CoupleFlow is intended to improve your sex life immediately, and also to promote enduring sexual satisfaction.*

satisfaction is to break through sexual barriers by engaging in new sexual activities. While it is generally accepted that experimenting with entirely new activities (assuming mutual desire to try them) can add welcomed variety to your sex life, it is certainly not the only way, and *may not actually be the best way*. One problem with the "breaking through barriers" approach is that there are only so many new tricks to be tried. You can vary positions, locations, lighting, accessories, control and risk, but at some point it might occur to you that you have reached the edge of your sexual universe.

But wouldn't it be great if you could have a new and different experience *in the moment,* even while engaging in a familiar activity? You would still feel free to experiment with new activities, yet without feeling obligated or expected to break new ground in the Bedroom. However, you would consistently find yourself in new territory because of how you are experiencing *that* particular moment. There is nothing routine about feeling a noticeably heightened connection while enjoying a mutually pleasurable experience with your loved one. So even if it seems like you have tried all the sexual activities you would like to try, that does not have to signify the end of your erotic exploration. In fact, if you believe as we do, that *each experience differs in some ways from any previous one*, this means that you will always be adding new pages to your pleasure menu.

Even in the Living Room, novelty is full of nuances. Sharing new experiences together is what got your relationship off the ground. Novelty was built into your early relationship with your partner simply because everything was new. But as your relationship matured, there were fewer and fewer "firsts" to be had, and seemingly less to discover about each other.

You may be aware of a recent best-selling book series that has captured millions of (mostly) women's longings -- not necessarily to be tied up and ravished by a handsome young billionaire, but to feel the sparks associated with early romance. The characters in the *50 Shades of Gray* series are so intensely drawn to each other in their developing relationship that you can feel the heat coming off the pages.

> *You can rekindle the behaviors that fueled your initial attraction to each other: noticing and flirting.*

So while it may be impossible to truly replicate the intoxicating early feelings of romantic relationships, you *can* rekindle the behaviors that fueled your initial attraction to each other: *noticing and flirting.*[6] Both women *and* men like to be noticed and known - for their talents, their passions, their insecurities, their contributions, their preferences, their attractiveness, and yes, for

---

[6] For elaboration on the stages of healthy courtship, we recommend Dr. Patrick Carnes' *Facing the Shadow* (Gentle Path Press, 2010), Chapter 3.

their erotic pleasures. It may not be as natural to notice such aspects in your partner after you've been together for years (or decades), but that is exactly what is required to enhance intimacy.

One couple's story along these lines involved an otherwise ordinary Sunday afternoon near the end of an ordinary weekend at home. Craig and Jessica had spent most of their waking hours together that weekend, whether it was running errands, shuttling their kids to birthday parties, or just taking care of all the usual household tasks. But when Craig and Jessica crossed paths in the kitchen on this particular afternoon, Craig suddenly turned around, took Jessica's hand, looked into her beautiful, blue eyes and said, "Hey, I don't think I've seen you this weekend." His gaze was met by Jessica's puzzled expression. "Sure, we've been *near* each other all weekend," Craig explained, "but I just realized I haven't really *seen* you. How *are* you? I'd really like to know." Jessica instantly felt more special to Craig than she had in a while, and it changed the complexion of the rest of the day. That night, they put the kids to bed a little earlier than usual and had the most Bedroom fun that either of them remembered in a long, *long* time.

Flirting is also something that usually fades away after early courtship. However, flirting is not just for young relationships. It may come more naturally for one of you than the other, but with a little

> *While the stuff of best-selling romance novels may be deliciously fictitious, the stuff of your own romance, as enriched via CoupleFlow, is powerfully real.*

thought, anyone can get back into the flirting game no matter how long you've been together. Remember what flirting is: playfully and/or sexily sending the message that you are most definitely *interested*. Innuendos, playfully touching, or giving your partner the look that says, "I am really digging you!" can do wonders for the circulation between your Living Room and Bedroom.

INTIMACY, NOVELTY AND VULNERABILITY

The variables that affect the experience of Sexual Abundance are *intimacy and novelty*, and both are fueled by *vulnerability*. Look at how these variables interact:

<u>**Figure 4:**</u>

<u>Sexual Abundance</u>

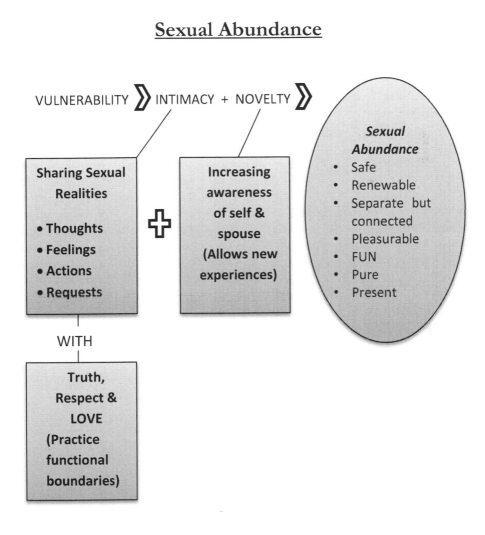

While Sexual Abundance emphasizes intimacy-based sexuality, it also promotes enjoying your pleasure to the fullest extent. Renowned psychoanalyst and sexuality expert, Dr. Michael Bader, endorses this perspective as he advocates for each person to "surrender to one's own selfish excitement without guilt or burdensome feelings of responsibility." Of course, he is not using the word "selfish" in the classic sense of the word, but as a means of emphasizing the importance of connecting with your own sexual reality during times of intimacy. To do this, it is necessary to let go of many of the thoughts that guide you in your non-sexual moments of life, such as when you are expected to be neat, quiet, contained, or deferential. You are then in a much better position to share your sexual realities with each other. However, all of this is done within the context of fully respecting each other and operating from a position of equality.

Sexual Abundance is characterized by consistent (not perfect) attunement, which is facilitated by staying firmly rooted in what is happening now -- for you *and* your partner. Examples of attunement include noticing and affirming each other, requesting something different, responding to such requests, making eye contact, being sensitive to each other's emotions, and tuning into your bodily sensations. Such moment-to-moment awareness promotes novelty, as each moment is different from any other and capable of being freely enjoyed. When experiencing this level of presence, you are very likely to feel gratitude (e.g., "This is a wonderful/special/warm/loving moment). And the state of mind we associate with gratitude is ... abundance.

As mentioned earlier, the *CoupleFlow* program will encourage you to risk some vulnerability by sharing your sexual realities with each other. That risk is rewarded each time you have a positive experience with your partner after allowing for some vulnerability.

Since this process of sharing sexual realities is so important, let's look at some specific examples:

- Sharing a *request:* "I'm wondering if you might want to shower together later tonight and see what happens."
- Sharing a *thought:* "I'm getting a little concerned that we haven't had much time together lately. Sometimes I tell myself that I shouldn't approach you when you have so much going on at work."
- Asking a *question:* "I know you've had a long day and I was wondering if you could use a hug or a backrub... or something a little more, um, *interesting?*"
- Sharing a *feeling,* "Last night was a *lot* of fun for me – I'm happy just thinking about our next time together and I have a lot of gratitude when I think about our love life."
- Taking an *action,* such as showing your partner exactly how you prefer to be touched or kissed.

Each of these types of sharing opens up a novel moment of connection which adds a new layer of intimacy. In the Bedroom, these can be every bit as connecting as trying a completely new sexual activity. What becomes new and different is how you are experiencing each other from one moment to the next. As a result, you end up with a new encounter, even if you are engaging in an "old" activity. Of course, there is nothing wrong with trying new activities. In fact, much of what you will be doing in this book is likely to be new.

A HOPEFUL LOOK AHEAD

Sidney and Aaron remarked during their *CoupleFlow* program that they noticed how different their kissing felt. As Sidney said, "It's not like he's doing much differently physically. It's more like I can *feel* him there with me, like he *wants* to be kissing me. It's not just kissing to cross it off the list so we can move on to the 'good parts.' I can tell he's more interested in me and how I'm enjoying the kiss. It's almost like we're kissing for the first time-again!"

Aaron was also aware of the differences: "In the past, I didn't think much about the kissing part. It was more of a stepping stone to what would come next. But it really helped to hear how much Sidney would like to enjoy kissing more; she put herself out there a little bit by telling me and I respect that. I'm realizing that I've also been missing out on the pleasure of kissing her. I just didn't know it. Now when we kiss it reminds me of how we kissed when we were dating -- and we've been married 14 years!"

As you move your relationship into a state of *CoupleFlow* and begin to experience Sexual Abundance, you may have some "I never" thoughts like some of our clients:

"I never knew how to ask for what I wanted."

"I never knew I could shed my inhibitions."

"I never knew I could be this present and connected with you during sex."

"I never knew you were so worried about disappointing me."

"I never knew you *had* any sexual preferences."

You don't need to become an expert in 57 Kama Sutra positions in order to breathe new life into your relationship and to revitalize your Bedroom. However, you can become more skilled in knowing your sexual realities and in deliberately sharing them with each other (Chapter Three will definitely give you a springboard in this regard).

SPIRITUALITY

We would be remiss to impart our *CoupleFlow* program without including the importance of spirituality in a loving relationship. Spirituality does not necessarily mean organized religion, though the major organized religions all are rooted in spirituality. Spirituality can take many forms. It can lead the way to joy and gratitude as well as wrap you in comfort during times of distress or uncertainty. Calling on God or your Higher Power or engaging in any form of spiritual practice (e.g., prayer/meditation) can absolutely help to strengthen your love for each other and your resilience.

Why is this so important? Because *every* relationship experiences challenge, struggle and the tendency to stagnate. A strong, shared spiritual connection can help you survive difficult stretches together, as perfectly imperfect partners living in an imperfect world. It can also raise your capacity for happiness, passion, pleasure and love. So when you consistently take time to connect with something greater than yourself and when you do so with your partner, you bond through your shared spiritual experience.

The physical act of sex itself is mechanically quite simple, yet the way you experience your sexual encounters can vary tremendously and contain multiple layers of complexity. On one end of the spectrum, you can feel emotionally disconnected even when physically satisfied. On the opposite end, you can feel *incredibly* connected through your Bedroom activities. This end of the spectrum is where you are likely to find a *spiritual connection* with your partner. There is a sacred feeling to the whole experience, fueled by your awareness that you are giving in to vulnerability, letting your guard down and leaving inhibitions behind. As you explore and savor each other's bodies and expand your passion, you are one with the moment, one with each other.

This is much more than a mechanical act, but a sanctified union of souls existing on a plane reserved exclusively for the two of you. You will have many opportunities to find yourselves in this highly desirable space in the *CoupleFlow* program, and each time you do, you'll feel love moving you toward each other. It is an experience that cannot be forced, but

> *This is much more than a mechanical act, but a sanctified union of souls existing on a plane reserved exclusively for the two of you.*

can be cultivated. By reading the rest of this book, you will establish for yourselves the most favorable conditions that consistently lead you toward moments you clearly recognize as spiritual.

WHAT WE CAN'T TELL YOU

Now that you have a general understanding of all that Sexual Abundance involves as well as how it fits within *CoupleFlow*, the rest of this book will guide you specifically through the *CoupleFlow* program. As clear as we are on what it takes to nurture a closely connected, energized and mutually satisfying Bedroom, we can't tell you *exactly* what your sexual intimacy should look like. We are simply going to give you a framework that supports the philosophy of Sexual Abundance and leave it to you to blend that framework into your unique relationship.

We sincerely hope that the ideas and exercises in this book get you thinking, talking and experimenting with a renewed spirit of partnership. But even if you read every page and try all the exercises in the exact order they appear, our hope is that you will come away with a strong sense of having used this book in a way that works *for you*, and inspired to continue seeking ideas and strategies that support your goals as a couple. As you move into Part Two of this book, you are on the verge of giving your relationship exactly what it needs to expand its potential and to thrive.

Part TWO

Making CoupleFlow Work for You

Introduction to Part Two

You are about to be guided through a series of steps that have been designed to rejuvenate your Bedroom connection as you simultaneously strengthen your Living Room connection. But before moving forward with Step One, consider some of the most common characteristics of couples with thriving relationships:

- They share a *clear vision* of their relationship thriving.
- They have a well-conceived *plan* to support their vision.
- They develop the necessary *mindset and skill set* required to deepen their intimacy.
- They build and strengthen a *framework* for discussing important issues that matter to each of them.
- They understand key concepts relating to *Sexual Abundance*, including *leaning in* to their vulnerabilities and *talking openly* about their sexual preferences.
- They know how to *protect their relationship* and they have a contingency plan in place to *repair* it when necessary.
- They avoid getting *stuck in resentment* due to fear-based interpretations and responses.
- They are consistently focused on *gratitude, joy and fun*.
- They always strive to be the *best possible partners to each other*, growing stronger each step of the way.

This book will give you clear guidance in strengthening each of these important areas. We offer six steps that will help you to pull a struggling relationship out of the storm clouds or to take an already satisfying relationship to new heights. No matter where you are starting from, you will benefit from this clear plan for establishing a connecting and energizing flow between your Living Room and Bedroom.

Each chapter contains clearly defined exercises called "Planned Intimate Experiences" or "PIEs." These PIEs will allow you to reinforce a solid core of emotional intimacy in the Living Room and to integrate an upgraded way of relating in the Bedroom. One question couples often ask us is, "How much time will each of these take?" Our general rule of thumb is to set aside about 30 minutes for each one. You may find that some of the communication PIEs take a little less time, while you may *want* to spend more than 30 minutes on some of the sensual and sexual PIEs. Either way, you will find it helpful to set aside a specific time for each PIE. Being intentional in this way demonstrates your commitment and allows you to build positive anticipation. You might even want to keep some activities on your calendars permanently – for instance, how bad can showering together every Sunday night be?

Erotic Intelligence[7]

As you move into the *CoupleFlow* program, you'll notice a graduated approach to sensual and sexual activities. In fact, it may seem to you that some of the early PIEs in this book are very basic. Your inner skeptic may ask, "Is it really necessary to talk about all this?" or "What's so great about caressing each other's backs?" The reality is that as simple as the key ingredients for relationship and sexual satisfaction can seem, it is very easy to lose sight of them. And when you lose sight of what it takes to make a relationship a wonderful place to be, you drift apart. Conversely, when you are intentional about taking steps known to be helpful, you *flow* together. So, *CoupleFlow's* emphasis on intentionality is quite intentional!

---

[7] We highly recommend Alex Katehakis's book, *Erotic Intelligence*, especially for individuals and couples in recovery from sex addiction.

But more than just "back to basics," many of the physical PIEs are included to purposefully heighten your sensual experience (and your bonding through shared pleasure) by approaching things a little differently. The cornerstone for many of these physical PIEs is a technique called *sensate focus*, originally developed by William Masters and Virginia Johnson, then furthered by Helen Singer Kaplan in the 1960's. Sensate focus involves a slowed-down, pressure-free approach to physically pleasuring each other so you can enjoy a higher quality connection to your senses during your times together (*translation: more pleasure!)*. Esther Perel so beautifully captures the fusion between the sensual and the erotic:

> *"We are born sensuous. And we become erotic. It is an intelligence that we cultivate and that stretches far beyond sex education. Erotic intelligence celebrates ritual and play, the power of imagination, and our infinite fascination with what is hidden, illicit and suggestive."*

Sensate focus is also a great way to promote one of the prerequisites for sexual arousal: *relaxation*. When you are *not* adequately relaxed and are experiencing anxiety, your sympathetic nervous system is triggered and your body directs blood away from your genitals and erogenous zones and toward your body's core. You are then prone to rushing through the act or having a less than desirable sexual response. A classic trigger for the sympathetic nervous system is when you find yourself monitoring your partner's or your own arousal. This is called "spectatoring" because it takes you out of your natural experience and puts you in the role of an outside observer (and a nervous one at that!).

But a relaxed body and mind is one which is primed and ready to experience pleasure in an uninhibited way. The parasympathetic nervous system is engaged and blood flows freely to your genitals and erogenous zones. You are very presently connected to your body's sensations and have given in to the moment. All this is to say that you may find yourself pleasantly surprised by how much you enjoy the slower approach of these sensate focus PIEs, and by how happy you are to have a more varied menu for pleasure. If so, you will have plenty of company.

If you came to our offices for traditional sex therapy, we would advise you to refrain from Bedroom activities that haven't yet been introduced in the program. This is a short-term strategy designed to support the overall goal of building a new way of connecting in the Bedroom through enhanced sensual awareness and pleasure. However, we know that this approach isn't for everyone. So if you do decide to use a PIE as foreplay to a lovemaking experience, we still encourage you to take it slowly. Do the PIE in its entirety before moving on to anything else, being mindful that these PIEs are not designed to be mere stepping stones to the "Main Event." Rather, they can be highly connecting and pleasurable encounters in and of themselves. As you are about to find out, each of them stands on its own.

GETTING STARTED

It can be quite helpful to decide in advance of each PIE not only the *where* and the *when*, but also the *who*, as in who will initiate the experience. The *initiator* is the person who calls your PIE time to order and prepares the room so it feels special. Room-prep can take many different forms and by no means needs to be elaborate. It might mean simply tidying up, or it could mean adjusting the room temperature and lighting, putting on some relaxing, fun or sexy music, having extra pillows or blankets on hand, etc. The basic idea is to create a nice little space to be physically affectionate with each other. Some refer to this as their "love nest," but whatever your lingo, it simply needs to feel right to the two of you. The structure of this system for initiating is designed to take any uncertainty and guesswork out of the process of getting started because nothing good can happen if you're not both in the same place at the same time and on the same page regarding what you are going to do (and if you are as busy as we are, then you know this is never an easy thing!). Here is an example of what it looks like in action.

Ryan and Tina agreed to set aside time for their next PIE on Wednesday at 9:30pm. As the initiator, Tina let Ryan know she was ready when it got to be 9:30, and told him she'd be waiting in the bedroom. When Ryan walked into the room a minute later, he noticed that instead of their usual overhead lighting and lamps, Tina had three scented candles burning. Tina had turned down the sheets and comforter and was smiling at him from the center of the bed, dressed in a negligee he had given her years ago and surrounded by the sweet sound of Sarah McLachlan playing in the background. As much as Ryan had thought that this "scheduling thing" was going to be a drag, all he could think of now was that he couldn't wait to get started! Tina read the instructions for the "Bedroom Soccer" PIE aloud as Ryan snuggled in next to her. Soon they were totally immersed with each other, laughing together, gazing at each other and pleasuring each other in ways they knew they would be coming back to again.

While Tina and Ryan were very intentional about how they set up their time together, what *actually happened* during their PIE was entirely organic. Yes, they had guidelines regarding the scope of the PIE, but every move they made and every wave of pleasure they had was entirely their own. After they finished, they would be able to discuss the questions at the end of the PIE (some couples even write their responses before sharing them with each other). Either option is a great way to get the most out of each PIE and to discuss whether you would like to add the entire PIE or any aspects of it to your Bedroom activities menu.

HOW TO ENJOY THE CARESSING PIEs

The caressing experiences are designed to build gradually upon each other in a wonderfully connecting and pleasurable way. During these experiences, you will take turns in the acts of giving and receiving pleasure through sensual and sexual touch. The type of touch being used in these PIEs is a *light, fingertips to skin caress* (not to be confused with a traditional massage which involves a deeper, more muscular rubdown).

Caressing each other in this way has two main benefits: First, your fingertips have an amazing capacity for pleasure -- both giving and receiving. You may already be familiar with this fact if you have enjoyed giving or receiving a slow, soft, lingering caress on any part of your body. Second, this type of gentle touch is a wonderful way to communicate your care, trust and nurturance for each other. A helpful visualization can be to imagine all of your feelings of affection, care and love flowing freely from your fingertips to the body of your partner.

Remember, there is no right or wrong way to caress or to receive a caress (though warm hands do help!) This is designed to be an interactive experience that is *structured but not scripted*: There are an endless number of possible experiences within the structure. Some people worry that the structure of scheduling and following instructions will eliminate any spontaneity. As was the case with Tina and Ryan, the structure simply gets you in the same place and on the same page. Every moment within that structured time is novel and no one else's except your own. There is plenty of room for spontaneity within the structure *as each of you is encouraged to verbalize anything that would make your experience more comfortable, pleasurable or fun.* Now we will review in detail each of the two roles that you will play during the caressing PIEs.

RECEIVER

As the receiver, your main goal is to soak up as much pleasure as possible, being mindful that *you are responsible for your own pleasure.* This involves a significant paradigm shift for many people who may have assumed that their *partner* was responsible for the quality of any given sensual or sexual experience. In fact, the most common sexual fantasy just might be, *"S/he should just know what I like!"* It's not that your partner's awareness is irrelevant, but even the most sensitive and attentive lover cannot know your mind and body as well as you. That is why it is so important to communicate (verbally and non-verbally) with your partner about what you would like more or less of.

The term used for asking for what you would like while being caressed is "redirection." An effective redirection often takes the form of teaching ("I'm really enjoying what you're doing, but could you please try using a circular touch *like this*?") Redirection does not always need to involve dialogue as sometimes a simple movement of your body or your partner's hand(s) will suffice.

> *The most common sexual fantasy just might be, "S/he should just know what I like!"*

Of course, when you are really enjoying being pleasured, a smile or a soft hum will definitely send the message you intend.

It is natural to experience some vulnerability when redirecting. This is because you are putting yourself out there ("This is how it feels good.") and asking someone to help you. As such, there is a good amount of trust involved. Not only are you are trusting that your partner will hear the redirection non-defensively, your partner is trusting that you *will* redirect whenever necessary. This is a much different process than *hoping* each other will "just know" what would feel good. It is also important that you not only ask directly for what you would like, but that you also have respect for your partner's response. For example, you might ask your partner if s/he could spend more time caressing your genitals, but your partner might be ready to move on to something else and would need to communicate this clearly to you. You would need to accept your partner's reality and not try to guilt or manipulate him/her into doing what you want.

The receiver should be able to press the "pause" button if s/he becomes uncomfortable (physically or emotionally) at any time and for any reason. If your relationship has had trust or sexual issues in the past, sometimes taking a break or switching roles can be helpful. (e.g., "I'm feeling a little anxious right now, so I think I'd like to just have you hold me and see how that feels" or "What you're doing feels so nice, but I can tell that I'm getting nervous again, so how about I caress you for a while to see how it goes?") Instead of

> *Slowing down to communicate clearly about sexual obstacles doesn't create distance; only staying silent about it does.*

being mood-killers, as many people fear, moments like these can be opportunities to enhance trust, acceptance and resonance. Slowing down to communicate clearly about sexual obstacles doesn't create distance; only staying silent about it does.

CARESSER

As the caresser, you will have the privilege of enjoying your partner's body in a very sensual way, using a light, fingertip to skin touch. Sometimes as the caresser you may feel uncertain regarding how to touch in a way that feels pleasurable to your partner. The best strategy is to *let your enjoyment of your partner's body guide your caressing.* This will allow you to be more presently connected with your own experience of the moment. There's nothing wrong with occasionally checking in with your partner

("Does this feel nice for you?") But it is also important to *trust that your partner is enjoying the caressing unless s/he offers a redirection.* When your partner *does* ask you to modify something, you can choose a gracious, generous and grateful spirit as you open yourself to your partner's request.

For some, this requires a shift in how you interpret your partner's redirection: It is *not* a critique (or a mandate), but a fully functional and necessary request for something different. It's also a sign of trust from your partner. It certainly does *not* mean you are doing anything wrong. For example, upon hearing your wife's request that you try a circular motion while caressing her rather than a vertical motion, instead of thinking, "I can never do anything right with her," or "Why does she always have to tell me what I'm doing wrong?" you can remind yourself that her request is about *her*, not about *you*. What *is* about you is that she trusts you enough to offer the redirection in the first place.

> *You can remind yourself that her request is about her, not about you.*

Before concluding this section, we offer guidance around a common question: "How much *time* should we spend in each role (caresser/receiver)?" We emphasize that having exactly equal amounts of time in each role is *not* as important as being as present as you can with each moment of your PIE time together. The only caveat is that it does take *some* time to really connect and to achieve a desired state of presence. The balance lies in allowing yourself *enough* time to connect as fully as possible in each role without feeling any time pressure.

In a relatively brief period of time, you'll be crossing the *CoupleFlow* finish line hand in hand. When you do, you'll have a system in place for ongoing enrichment and enjoyment of your relationship strengths. You will consistently find abundant joy in your relationship and you'll know better than ever how to intentionally create the flow that works best for you. Congratulations on embarking on this journey and enjoy the ride!

Chapter One

CoupleFlow Step One:
Protect to Connect

Think for a moment about all the things you protect. You make sure your children have car seats, helmets, proper nutrition and safety knowledge. You get an annual physical exam and use sunscreen when you go outside. You have property insurance, life insurance and car insurance. You keep your valuables in a safe place and make sure your doors are locked and the security system is on before going to bed. You keep your pets' shots up to date. Why do you take these steps? Because each of these areas represents something that is important to you and it is in your best interest to protect it.

Now think about your relationship. Is there anything more important to you than that? That's why the first rule of thumb in the *CoupleFlow* program is *protect your relationship.* Couples who intentionally protect their relationship day in and day out set themselves up for relationship excellence. So when it comes to protecting relationships, there are three primary components that require active protection: *respect* for each other, *time* with each other, and *fidelity* to each other. The last two may seem obvious, but without mutual respect, no relationship can flourish. This chapter will give

> *Couples who intentionally protect their relationship set themselves up for relationship excellence.*

you clearly structured PIEs to strengthen your ability to protect these core components of intimate relationships.

RESPECT

Relationships characterized by abundance and ongoing, deepening satisfaction tend to be similar along one major theme: Each partner consistently respects the other and themselves in their thoughts, words and behaviors. The benefits of living respectfully are vast and limitless. One of those benefits is preservation of the vision you have defined, because without respect, even the most beautifully articulated vision is destined to be unfulfilled.

What we commonly refer to as boundaries provide the system that facilitates respectful living. While healthy boundaries may come more naturally for some than for others, living respectfully as a way of life by consistently utilizing a system of healthy boundaries requires a *very specific skill set*. In fact it may be THE most important skill set you have never been taught. Given how little time most of us spend learning the skills associated with meaningful, connected, passionate, safe and enduring relationships, you would almost think they weren't that important! Can you think of anything else in life where something is so

> *What we commonly refer to as boundaries provide the system that facilitates respectful living.*

highly valued, often with so many consequences when things go poorly, but where there is typically so little attention paid to developing the relevant skill set?

The following section on boundaries will add a significant source of strength to your relationship. Even if you've had little or no training until now (or the *wrong* kind of training), it is entirely possible to learn and practice the skills you need to live respectfully and to share yourselves in truth and love with each other. It is exactly what is called for in order to make your vision for relationship excellence a reality.

Boundaries

You might be familiar with a well-known adage, *"Good fences make good neighbors."* The idea is in relationships it helps to have a clear idea about where your stuff ends and where another's begins. More than a mere property line, practicing healthy boundaries in relationships helps you to deepen your emotional intimacy while holding onto your sense of self. Boundaries allow you the moment-to-moment awareness that *you* are in charge of your thoughts and feelings, regardless of what is swirling around you. Boundaries give you the

> *More than a mere property line, practicing healthy boundaries in relationships helps you to deepen your emotional intimacy while holding onto your sense of self.*

presence of mind to decide who is safe enough to let in and with whom you need to be more careful.

This much we know from our personal experience: *The model of healthy boundaries that we present in this section can do more to change unhealthy relationship dynamics (or improve already good ones) than anything else we know of.* You'll end up with the best of both worlds: connection and protection. In this model, mutual respect defines your interactions and promotes the kind of sharing which results in emotional intimacy.

First, we'd like you to think of your personal boundary system as a two-way filter that surrounds you. In one direction it protects you from whatever is coming toward you from others. For example, when you are listening to your partner talking, your boundary allows you to know that everything you are hearing is about *your partner*. You remain in touch with your reality even as you are tuned into your partner's reality. You are listening for the simple purpose of *knowing your partner's reality*. You are not listening to judge your partner's reality or to control it in any way. For example, consider the experience of Jack and Maya:

Maya had been very eager to plan a trip with her husband and three young children to visit her family, who lived on the opposite coast of the U.S. She had not seen them in more than a year, and had mentioned on several occasions to Jack that she hoped to make this happen during the upcoming holidays. Jack's response was brief: "Sounds good. We should talk more about it." One night, Maya approached Jack with an interest in making some definite plans. "I was hoping we could look at the calendar and see how we could visit my family during the holidays. Do you have a few minutes to take a look with me?" "Sure," Jack responded, "but I'd like to discuss a few concerns before we look at dates."

Jack and Maya thereby arrived at an intersection with several divergent paths before them, and with each path dependent on their respective boundaries. If Maya's boundaries were working for her, she would remind herself that whatever Jack was about to share, it could be a real opportunity. It would give them a chance to talk through his concerns directly and to negotiate around any differences. If her boundaries were *not* working properly, she would be vulnerable to overreacting to Jack's reality, fearful that she would not be heard or that her wants would not be deemed important.

When your boundary system is working, you know that you can handle whatever your partner shares with you, even if it is intense or completely different from your perspective. That's because your boundary allows you to only take in and have feelings about that which *you* choose. You become the watch guard for your thoughts and feelings. No one can victimize you or *make you feel anything unless you sign off on it*. This leaves you in a position to respond without defensiveness, because once you have accepted that you are merely hearing a different perspective, you have nothing to defend. You have no investment in convincing your partner that s/he is wrong (or that you are right). You feel perfectly free to have a different perspective and are hopeful that you can negotiate compromise around any decisions that need to be made. And while you cannot control any intensity that your partner may be experiencing, you *can* control whether you choose to feed into it or to remain even and respectful.

In the other direction, when you are talking, your filter ensures that you are communicating your reality with your partner in a moderate and respectful way. You are sharing with the simple purpose of letting your partner know what *your reality* is. How your partner hears what you share is largely beyond your control. In fact, the only variables you control are how clearly and respectfully you are communicating. With this in mind, it is easier to let go of the outcome of your interaction. If your partner has a different perspective, then you will need to respect it, avoid taking anything personally and negotiate if your preferences differ or a decision needs to be made. Of course, it makes things a lot easier when you get a mature, respectful response. However, if your partner gives you less than a mature response, that just means you will need to step up by handling *yourself* maturely. To illustrate the value of practicing healthy boundaries when you are talking, let's look at Karen's surprise dinner for Paul:

Shortly after they were married, Karen prepared what she thought would be a very special dinner for Paul. She went to her favorite market, splurged on the freshest, highest quality ingredients and even bought flowers and candles for the table. When Paul got home, the flowers were on the table, the candles were lit, their favorite music was playing and the meal was ready. He couldn't believe it. No one had ever done anything quite like this for him before! Karen happily set a beautifully prepared plate in front of Paul and joined him at the table. As they de-briefed about their days and talked excitedly about their upcoming weekend plans, Karen could not help noticing that Paul had barely touched his shrimp stir-fry entrée. After a few more minutes of watching him eat everything on his plate except the shrimp, her facial expression changed from pleasant to annoyed. "What is it?" he asked. "Well I guess I spent all this time cooking the wrong meal. You haven't even touched your shrimp!" Karen curtly responded.

At this moment, if Paul had his boundaries working for him, he would say something like this: "Karen, I can tell you put so much thought and effort into this dinner. It's obvious how special you wanted this to be for me, so I wasn't sure how to say this... but I had shrimp at a lunch meeting today. They weren't very good and that's why I'm just not hungry for shrimp right now. I loved everything else, especially the fried rice, but I can understand if you're disappointed."

Now if Karen really had her boundaries working for *her,* she would be able to hear Paul's reality without taking personally the fact that he wasn't hungry for shrimp. She might be disappointed (and who wouldn't be?) but she would not *need* Paul to enjoy the shrimp in order for her to still feel good about the experience she had created for them (and certainly not to feel good about *herself*). If she was really on her game she might playfully tell him, "Well I hope you didn't have any bad brownie sundaes for lunch because that's what coming out for dessert!" She would not let Paul's lunch get in the way of her dinner with him.

Communicating Like Adults

When couples come to our office, the most commonly cited problem is "communication difficulties." Almost without exception, the reason for this problem is that they have been limiting themselves to the *Children's Menu* of options for their interactions. Reaching for the Children's Menu can happen in a flash -- something happens or is said and all of a sudden the prefrontal cortex of your brain cedes control to the significantly less evolved limbic system. At that point, you engage in the kinds of interpretations, thoughts and feelings that you did when you were much younger. In that state of mind, you are one with your emotions and likely to choose options from the Children'sMenu.

Notice the difference between the following menus:

Children's Menu	Adults' Menu
• Avoid • Attack (self/others) • Defend • Enmesh	• Use boundaries for protection & connection • Share your truth moderately • Listen respectfully • Accept reality before acting • Decide when to attach feelings • Own responsibility for feelings • Express anger thoughtfully • Negotiate compromise • Decide who is safe and who is not • Take a break when overwhelmed • Ask directly for what you want • Answer directly when asked • Appreciate and accept partner's "no"

As you can see, the children's menu has very few options and none of them is very appealing.

- **Avoid**: Kids are expert avoiders from the time they first avert their gaze from the knowing eyes of a parent who has caught them in some act of misbehavior. Along the way, they learn (and are taught) to avoid their negative feelings too. Examples include: "You shouldn't be upset about that." "Don't cry." "Why are you making such a big deal out of this?" Many children learn to shut down when faced with uncomfortable feelings, withdrawing into their own worlds to escape the pain of the world around them.

- **Attack**: Kids attack others and themselves when under duress. Even a four year old has an arsenal of names to call whoever happens to be frustrating him. By age six, children can unleash a flood of critical commentary toward anyone in their path. By then, children also tend to turn negative emotions (shame, guilt, anger, pain) inward on themselves. The cycle of lashing out, then lashing in begins very early.

- **Defend**: This option goes hand in hand with the previous one. "It's not my fault!" "No, *you* are wrong!" "This wouldn't have happened if..." "Yeah well s/he started it!" The art of aggressive defense and shifting blame is learned before a child enters Kindergarten.

- **Enmesh**: This is where children are too invested in other people's perceptions of them. They spend much energy and focus on garnering approval and staying in the good graces of the people who matter most in their lives. They are more aware of what these people are thinking and feeling and doing than they are of themselves. One of the classic pathways to enmeshment involves a child feeling responsible for a parent's emotional/physical well-being. These kids grow up to be emotional caretakers, love avoidants and/or worriers.

Compare the limited options on the Children's Menu to the wide range of empowering options on the Adults' Menu.

- **Use boundaries for protection and connection:** Boundaries allow the best of both worlds in healthy adult relationships- protection and connection. Thus, each partner's individuality is valued within the context of a deeply intimate relationship. Boundaries support respectful negotiation around differences and grace toward self and others.

- **Share your truth *moderately*:** Adults understand that their perspective is not the only important perspective. They also know that they do not need approval or agreement in order for their perspective to be valid. This reduces intensity and allows for the kind of even-handed communication that their partner is most likely to hear non-defensively. The spirit of sharing is to let your partner know where you stand -- your thoughts, feelings and any requests you have. Sharing these truths is an act of intimacy, not persuasion.

- **Listen respectfully:** Listening from an adult frame of mind allows you to stay tuned into your partner's perspective without losing your own. You can appreciate that your partner is choosing to let you in and may be feeling vulnerable even if there are no overt signs of vulnerability. You can let your partner have his/her thoughts and feelings about any given thing while reminding yourself, *"This is about my partner- I do not need to judge what I am hearing or try to change it. I may offer my own perspective in response, knowing that each of our perspectives have equal value, regardless of their differences."*

- **Accept reality before acting:** Acceptance does not necessarily mean *liking* your circumstances. It means being real enough with yourself to acknowledge: "This is how things are right now." From this non-judgmental, reality-based perspective, you can then assess your options. Slowing down enough to gain clarity before acting is usually a strong option.

- **Decide when to attach feelings:** Unlike children, who typically react instantly based on their feelings, adults can learn to detach in healthy ways from their emotions and the emotions of others. This does not mean they do not feel. Instead, they observe their feelings as they arise, and try to understand where they are coming from. They learn that while strong feelings can arise quickly, they do not always warrant action.

- **Own responsibility for feelings:** When feelings arise, adults know that those feelings belong to them and no one else. Because their boundaries are more developed than children's, they do not blame others for their feelings (e.g., "You're making me feel guilty"). With rare exception, adults make themselves feel whatever they are feeling in response to interactions with others. Understanding this helps you avoid victim thinking and promotes relating from an equal position.

- **Express anger thoughtfully:** Anger is a secondary emotion arising from fear, pain, and shame. It can give us strength to set limits with others, but it can also appear as resentment, or victim-anger. Unlike children, adults can learn to understand where their anger is originating. Is it here in the present, based solely on something offensive or disrespectful that just happened? Or is it fueled by the past, adding intensity and distorted interpretations of others' motivations? The answer allows adults to know whether to use their anger as an asset or to attend to the old fears, shame and/or pain that are being triggered.

- **Negotiate compromise:** Kids argue with one goal in mind: to win. Adults can recognize differing perspectives and desired outcomes without going all out in order to emerge victorious. Instead, they can respect that two different people will naturally have different preferences and ideas about all kinds of things. Adults do not perceive their partner as a threat upon recognizing such differences. They honor their partner's perspectives just as they do their own and they negotiate compromise in good faith to the best of their abilities.

- **Decide who is safe and who is not:** Children are thrown into this world -- into their family, their peer group and their classrooms. They do not have the luxury of choosing to invest only in relationships that are good for them. Adults do, and benefit greatly from realizing and exercising their right to decide with whom to be vulnerable on a case by case basis and to allow for those assessments to shift over time.

- **Take a break when overwhelmed:** Kids often don't realize when they are approaching the limits of their emotional reserves. They are therefore more prone to over-reacting, misinterpreting and shutting down. An adult frame of mind allows you to recognize when you are overextended and to take appropriate self-care steps.

- **Ask directly for what you want:** This runs counter to the fantasy that begins at a very young age that "others should know what I want." Adults recognize this kind of thinking as a recipe for disappointment. A more mature approach involves accepting that others cannot be expected to know what you prefer unless you articulate it clearly. Hints, innuendo and hoping may work occasionally, but asking directly gives your partner the best chance to respond to your requests.

- **Answer directly when asked for something:** You probably prefer to know where you stand with others rather than feeling uncertain. When your partner honors you with a direct request, you can honor your partner with a clear reply. Perhaps you can agree to the request, perhaps not (or not right now), but either way, everyone is better served with a straight answer.

- **Appreciate and accept "no" from your partner:** It's never easy to make a request of your partner and then to not get the response you were hoping for. At times like these, an adult mindset allows you to not take your partner's unavailability personally and to appreciate that your partner is practicing self-care by not overextending him/herself.

*****

The following PIE gives you a chance to assess your own tendencies toward the Children's and Adults' menus.

Which Menu Will You Be Ordering From Today?

> *"There's no better feeling than knowing we can talk about absolutely anything."*
> *-Claire, 39*

Why This Matters:

All of the interactions that take place between you and your partner begin as thoughts or interpretations, which can quickly give rise to feelings. The thought to feeling cycle happens over and over and can take place in less time than it took to read a single word in this sentence. These initial thoughts and feelings may not always serve you and your partner well because many times, they are the same automatic reactions you had as a child. In fact, one of the most common recipes for relationship dissatisfaction is trying to have an adult relationship but doing so through child-like ways of relating. This is all done unintentionally, of course, but the antidote is as intentional as it gets: Learning to identify and inhibit your natural tendencies toward the Children's Menu and to deliberately choose from the Adults' Menu, where the healthiest and most satisfying options are always found.

Guidelines:

Circle the items you tend toward on the Children's Menu (on page 62), then write at least one example for each one. Also note how these options work for you. Then take a look at the Adults' Menu: Place an "S" next to any you would identify as strengths and a "G" next to those you assess as growth areas. Choose a time to share your responses with each other.

Adult to Adult Communicating

> *"What's amazing to me is how much farther we can go in our conversations."*
> *-Jonathan, 46*

Why This Matters:

The communication model outlined below has been designed to bring the previously discussed boundary principles down to a practical level. You can use this model for any conversation, but it is especially helpful when you find yourself in some emotionally dicey territory. Using the following communication model will help you to slow down in order to:

- think about what you want to communicate
- say it in a way that your partner is most likely to hear
- listen respectfully while holding onto your own reality
- speak and listen from a position of equality

This model will keep you on the Adults' Menu despite any tendencies toward the Children's Menu. It might not feel natural at first, but it will also allow you to go deeper in your discussions, helping them become more meaningful and safe.

Guidelines:

First, read the guidelines for *Adult to Adult Communicating* on the following pages out loud together. Be sure to use specific feeling words when sharing feelings. Here are the Big 8:

LOVE	PASSION	JOY	FEAR
ANGER	SHAME	GUILT	PAIN/SADNESS

Using your *Internal Talking Boundary* as you share your reality:

SPEAKER: Your goal is to *let your partner know your perspective at this moment.* It is not to manipulate, control, or persuade that yours is the *correct* perspective. While maintaining an equal and respectful position and engaging your *talking boundary*, you begin with a REQUEST, end with a REQUEST, and have three SHARES in the middle. Before sharing, consider what it would be like if your partner used the same approach with you that you are about to use with him/her.

1. **REQUEST time**: *"There is something I'd like to share with you. Is now a good time?"* If the answer is "yes" proceed to #2. If the answer is no, ask, *"When do you think might be a better time?"*

2. **SHARE what happened**: What did you hear or see or experience that you'd like your partner to know? (*"When we were talking at the table you got up and left without saying anything and you had a tense look on your face."*)

3. **SHARE your thoughts** about what happened: What meaning did you give to what happened? We highly recommend using a phrase like, *"What I made up about that was..."* or *"What I perceived was..."* Using language such as this allows you to take ownership of your reality while leaving plenty of room for your partner's perspective. It will steer you clear of making outright negative assumptions and/or blaming your partner for *making* you feel a certain way. (*"So I made up that you were upset with me, but I'm not sure why."*)

4. **SHARE the emotions** that relate to your thoughts: (*"I have some fear that if you are upset with me, you will avoid me. I also have some pain and anger- pain because it feels like an old pattern being repeated again, and anger because that felt disrespectful to me."*)

5. **REQUEST** what you would like from your partner. We recommend framing your requests as preferences, as opposed to needs, unless it *really* is a need. This keeps you in touch with your power to care for yourself while making requests. Also, when someone hears your request as a preference, s/he is more likely to be receptive. (*"I'd like to request that you not leave so abruptly when we are talking. If you feel like you do need to leave, I'd appreciate you letting me know that and telling me when you'll be back."*)

Using Your *Internal Listening Boundary* to hear your partner and respond:

RECEIVER: You have one primary goal when your partner shares his/her reality with you: You are listening *to learn more about your partner's perspective and experience.* As you listen, you are in a position to help your partner feel understood by making eye contact, listening carefully, and not interrupting. Use the following steps:

1. **CHECK YOURSELF** by remembering that your partner is *trusting you* by sharing thoughts, feelings and requests. Everything you are hearing is *about your partner*, though it probably involves you. And as you respect your partner's reality, you also stay connected with your own reality. No matter what you hear, you will respond in a respectful way, even if it involves setting a limit.

2. **RECOGNIZE what you partner shared** by paraphrasing what you heard. Then go as far as you can in your partner's direction while remaining authentic. (*"I hear that you had a reaction to the way I left the room. You saw something on my face and you had some feelings -- pain, fear and anger -- come up for you. I also heard your request about how I can do things differently. First, thank you for letting me know this. As you explained how it was for you, I could understand how you'd be feeling those things."*)

3. **SHARE your reality** as it relates to what your partner has shared. Can you relate and do you agree with what you have just heard? If not, you probably would like to clarify your perspective or seek more information from your partner to enhance your understanding of his/her perspective. (*"I think I understand where you're coming from, but I want to clarify something also. Would that be OK?"*)

4. **RESPOND directly** to your partner's request. Look for any part of it you can say "yes" to. Also be clear about what you cannot agree to, or if you would like some time to consider the request (*"I can certainly be more aware of how that kind of thing affects you and I can definitely let you know when I need to leave the room in the future."*). Avoid using phrases such as "In my defense…" or "As I've told you before…" There is no need to defend or remind if you are maintaining a position of equality with your partner.

Boundaries Make the Bedroom Grow Warmer?

Being mindful of these communication principles can also pay big dividends with your sexual intimacy. As important as it is to discuss your sexual realities, a safety net needs to be in place to regulate the experience and flow of your perceptions and feelings. These boundaries you have been reading about *are* that safety net.

It certainly helps to have a partner who operates

> *These communication principles can also pay big dividends with your sexual intimacy.*

within the same communication model, but it can be quite empowering to any individual regardless of your partner's practice.

Here's how this all works in the Bedroom: Say you would like a different kind of touch or a different progression of touch. If your boundaries are working for you, you will be relating to your partner from a position of equality, respect and trust. Thus, you could state your reality to your partner as follows: "Honey, I really like it when you rub my _____ (fill in the blank). Next time, do you think you could try a softer touch? I'd really like that." Contrast this with a boundary-less approach communicated from an unequal perspective: *"How many times do I have to tell you to use a lighter touch? It's seriously like talking to the wall!"*

Practicing adult communication not only promotes respectful discussions about sexual preferences, but also helps with one of the top sources of sexual conflict among couples -- availability. It gets tricky when you try to initiate something sexual and then receive a version of "no" in response. The "no" in and of itself is not inherently problematic -- it's just a normal part of being in a relationship. What becomes problematic is when the person who initiated goes beyond feeling disappointed by taking the response personally, as a *rejection*, and becomes resentful.

The solution lies with using the Adults' Menu to respectfully communicate when you are not available (e.g., "I'm sorry I don't think I'm up for anything right now, because of XYZ, but I do think tomorrow would be better. That way, we'll have more time and I'll have more energy than I do right now. How would that be for you?") The same menu also allows you to avoid taking your partner's unavailability personally. You can appreciate and accept your partner's "no" while giving him/her room to say "yes" to another time and to

> *You need the freedom to be authentic, whether it is saying "no" without fear of consequence or "yes" with enthusiasm.*

mean it. This approach incorporates a cornerstone of healthy sexuality: mutual consent. Each of you needs the freedom to be authentic, whether it is saying "no" without fear of consequence or "yes" with enthusiasm. If you do notice a pattern of sexual avoidance that concerns you, your boundaries allow you to express that respectfully as well.

This communication model not only enhances discussions about sexuality, but it helps you have deeper, more connecting conversations in general. You know that experience when you realize you are really getting each other, or that you just talked

~ 87 ~

through something that previously would have ended in conflict? It's exhilarating and can even be a turn-on! But there's nothing sexy about trying to have an adult conversation with someone who is stuck on the Children's Menu.

It might seem paradoxical, but *practicing healthy boundaries actually allows for greater closeness*. Here's the logic: Boundaries promote respect, respect promotes safety, and safety promotes honesty. With healthy boundaries, you can honestly let your partner know what your truth is, and you can hear your partner's truth without becoming lost or defensive. Mutual sharing in this way is the *heart of intimacy*. When each of you consistently follows the path (marked by boundaries) that leads to the Adults' Menu, you will notice an improved ability to share your sexual realities with each other and will

> *Practicing healthy boundaries actually allows for greater closeness.*

increase the likelihood of experiencing a much richer sexual intimacy than ever before. Few things pave the way for adult pleasure as powerfully as adult communication does. The next PIE allows you to build in time for connecting as adults on a daily basis.

Daily Shares

Why This Matters:

This PIE was developed with busy couples in mind, giving you a very efficient way to notice and connect with each other -- in as little as *five minutes*. Sometimes, you may find yourselves going beyond five minutes, choosing to discuss some parts of your Daily Shares in greater detail. There is also something to be said for the process of "just showing up" as you keep this commitment to each other. Each time you follow through and make yourself available you send a message: "This time is important to me, because *you* are important to me." This helps to solidify your bond as partners who are in this together.

Guidelines:

- First, agree to meet at a specific time near the end of the day or evening. Eventually you may have a set time each evening for your Daily Shares, but in the beginning you might want to experiment to see what works best. This process also can work fine over the phone if you cannot meet in person.
- Take turns sharing with the other using the following format[8]:

---

[8] Virginia Satir developed "Daily Temperature Taking" for a similar purpose and in a similar format, though with some different topics of focus. For more, visit http://www.pairs.com/dtr.php

1. **Express an affirmation**. The only criterion for this affirmation is that it is a positive statement that is true for you. Examples:

- *"I appreciate your work ethic, especially lately."*
- *"I really admire how you handled that situation even though it must not have been easy."*
- *"I've been feeling really good about us, and it has a lot to do with how you…"*
- *"You looked so amazing when we were out the other night."*
- *"I really felt close to you when you put your arm around me last night."*
- *"I think you have the greatest laugh – and you smell great, too!"*
- *"When you considered my request to change plans instead of just saying "no," I really appreciated your flexibility.*

2. **Share something from your day.** It could be something that feels big, or perhaps something that feels light or even trivial. Examples:

- *"I ran into Melissa when I was at lunch and I realized how much I miss her friendship."*
- *"I tried calling the computer support line again but they made me wait forever and I had to hang up before I was even able to talk with anyone -- so I was really frustrated and I'm starting to worry that it will never get fixed."*
- *"I overheard Caleb explaining to Mackenna that the tooth fairy will only leave money under the pillow if the tooth doesn't have any cavities. They are so funny sometimes!"*

3. **Share something that's on your radar: A hope, dream, vision or concern.** It could be something way off on the horizon, or something that is with you right now. Examples:
- *"I'm really looking forward to our date on Friday."*
- *"I'm starting to think more about changing my career path."*
- *"It's going to be great to see Anne tomorrow -- I've really missed her."*
- *"As we get closer to the school year starting, I can feel my anxiety building."*

4. **Share a request you have of your partner.** There may be times when you don't have any burning requests, but you should try to come up with *something*. Requests involve at least some degree of vulnerability, which is so important in raising your intimacy potential. Requests can also take the form of asking your partner to continue doing something that is helpful to you. Examples:
- *"It would mean a lot to me if you could remember to pick up your socks and underwear from the floor before you go to work."*
- *"Every time you call me from work it helps me feel loved and appreciated -- please keep doing that!"*
- *"I know I've asked this before, but I'd really like you to hear me this time... I want you to stop talking about our money issues in front of the kids. Can you please wait until we have privacy to have those discussions? It would mean a lot to me."*

*****

We challenge you to do these Daily Shares consistently for 10 days. We can just about guarantee you that you will notice an enhanced connection and that you will want to continue this dedicated way of connecting at the end of your day.

TIME

One of the first challenges many couples notice in beginning this program is the need to find time with each other to actually complete the Planned Intimate Experiences. As a society, we are busier than at any other time in history, so it has never been more challenging (and therefore never more important) to protect your time together. We have yet to meet the couple that starts the *CoupleFlow* program and says, "We're so glad that we now have something to do with all the spare time we had laying around!" The time has to come from somewhere, and you will likely need to negotiate times to which you can both agree. Your ability to plan your PIE time consistently with each other will directly affect your level of success in this program and in an ongoing way in your relationship. We don't call them PLANNED Intimate Experiences for nothing!

Some of you might ask, "What about spontaneity?" Let us be clear on two things: 1. Spontaneity is overrated, and 2. There is plenty of room for your entirely natural, unprompted experiences within the time you deliberately set aside to be together. While relying primarily on spontaneity usually yields *less* total quality time together, planned time provides the most basic ingredients for any meaningful, fun, pleasurable, couple experiences…you're both in the same place at the same time, ready for the same thing! Whatever happens after that does not need to be boring or canned. Even within the structure of these PIEs, there is no limit on your authentic, spur of the moment responses and interactions.

> *As a society, we are busier than at any other time in history.*

Everything that takes place during a planned time together is every bit as real as during a spontaneous time together. So, the moral of

> *Leave room for spontaneity, but protect your planned time like your relationship depends on it – because it does.*

the story is, leave room for spontaneity but protect your planned time together like your relationship depends on it -- because it does.

FIDELITY

If two people are really in love with each other and really care for each other, then that must mean they are immune from infidelity, right? Not so fast. The truth of the matter is that *no one* gets a free pass on fidelity. We are all vulnerable to some form of infidelity, just by virtue of our human nature. Maybe you know yourself well enough to know that there are certain things that you would just never do. Nevertheless, just because you don't see yourself waking up in bed with someone else under any circumstances, there are many ways you can still be proactive in reinforcing fidelity to your partner. The following sections detail some of the many areas that may seem harmless enough at first glance, but that can turn into fidelity minefields.

Opposite Sex Friends (or same sex if homosexual)

We know a married woman who has more male friends than most guys do. She is always going places with them (shopping, hiking, art shows, happy hours, etc.), texting, calling, and making plans. We don't doubt her faithfulness (that's not our place or anyone else's), but sometimes we can't help but wonder how she ever has time for her husband! Having opposite sex friends isn't wrong, but there is one undeniable truth to bear in mind: All friendships require energy-- *emotional* energy. The reality is that we do not have a bottomless supply of this precious commodity so we need to be very intentional about where and how we invest it. This is especially true when considering that the feedback loop between the Living Room and Bedroom of your relationship that leads to Sexual Abundance *runs on emotional energy*. So ask yourself: *"Where is my emotional energy going these days? How much am I directing into the relationship that means the most to me? Are there any relationships that are draining off some of my emotional energy that otherwise would be available to my partner?"*

Working Closely with Opposite Sex Colleagues

Sometimes this just can't be avoided. In fact, it doesn't *need* to be avoided in most situations. However, there are three instances when it should definitely be treated with caution:

1. You recognize YOU have some feelings of attraction for a colleague.

This isn't wrong and doesn't mean your relationship is in trouble. Sometimes they're just feelings, and you certainly can decide not to act on them. But when they *are* there, you need to take some precautions: Don't flirt. Don't have one on one lunches, dinners, coffees or drives alone together. Don't discuss details from your marriage or committed relationship (other than to make it known you are in one!) Dishing about one's relationship hardships is usually the first domino to fall in any developing workplace affair.

2. You recognize a COLLEAGUE has feelings for you.

Apply the same precautions as in #1, and be ready to set clear limits if anything becomes overtly flirtatious or otherwise inappropriate.

3. You don't recognize anything…but your partner sure does!

Sometimes your partner will notice and pick up on things that you do not. Little things, perhaps, but they set off your partner's radar and s/he tells you their concerns. Listen. Do not try to talk your partner out of their perceptions and feelings. Just tell the truth ("I'm not aware of any feelings toward Mandy.") and let your partner know you respect his/her feelings. If your partner's observations result in *you* noticing something, ("By golly, Mandy *does* flirt with me!") the best course of action is to be upfront about it ("I can see why you'd think that, and to be honest, maybe I have been a little too unaware of how she's coming across... I'll be handling things differently from now on.")

Business Travel

Traveling for business can create the illusion of a parallel universe, where normal rules do not apply. Staying in a hotel room hundreds or thousands of miles away from one's family is a lonely experience. Combine loneliness with the stress of the business meeting or conference, and then combine those feelings with alcohol. Now we've just moved into some potentially risky territory. Increasing the risk is the fact that there are others in the same boat at the same meeting or conference in the same hotel who are similarly vulnerable. Even if you have never cheated or felt tempted, it never hurts to remind oneself that while the surroundings may be different, your commitments to your partner are *constant* travel companions.

Flirting

World-renowned sexuality researcher and author, Dr. Patrick Carnes, has defined flirting as "high intensity, low-commitment behavior." In other words, flirting involves sending a message that one has romantic interest in another person, but without any risk of attachment. It may seem so innocent, and the word "flirting" has such a light and airy feel to it! But when flirting, you *are* stepping back from your committed relationship and toward someone else, even if just for a moment. When viewed this way, it is clearly not in the spirit of protecting one's relationship. And the worst case scenario is that the innocent flirting may be a stepping stone to a more obvious breach of fidelity.

Complaining About Your Partner

This is perhaps the most common breeding ground for just about any affair. It may seem innocent or humorous to make a reference to some complaint about your partner especially if it's done in a humorous way. But you may be sending a signal that you're unhappy at home. You can protect your relationship by agreeing to never utter an ill word about your partner or your relationship to an opposite sex person.

Physical Touch with an Opposite Sex Person

We're not talking about a hello hug if that's your style and your partner is OK with it. The type of touch that can become problematic might look casual, but can also introduce the possibility of unexpected feelings arising out of it. For example, Bob never thought of Sandy as a love interest, but one day when she playfully touched his arm while they were talking, he suddenly felt a wave of sexual energy pass through him -- nothing he was worried about acting on, but it sure did get his attention. He realized that he needed to sit a little further away from her in the future because he did not want to be in that position again.

Technology (Social Networking, Texting, Tweeting, Gaming, TV, etc.)

There can be no denying technology's recent and significant impact on relationships. The increased opportunity for self-expression in so many new forums provides round the clock, up to the second connection with others' lives. If you think about how it all burst onto the scene around the turn of the 21st century, that was already a time in our culture when we were maxed out on sleep deprivation, overwork and overextension of all kinds. The time and energy required to keep up with everyone's Facebook or Twitter or Instagram or Pinterest posts or to monitor the steady stream of emails and texts to your smart phone does not come from a limitless supply -- it is finite, so it comes at the expense of investing it elsewhere... like in the relationship that matters *most* to you.

While the jump in technology has allowed us all to have more "friends" who "like" us than ever, it is also true that these new forums for connecting *can* be more like entertainment than intimacy. Additionally, there is often an illusion that what happens in cyberspace exists in some sort of bubble, detached from real life. Many an affair has had its birthplace in a seemingly innocent connection with an old friend (or a new one). The risk in these situations increases when one (often quite unconsciously or unintentionally) goes looking for a "connection fix." The person's romantic relationship is not meeting their intimacy needs, and an endless array of options for some form of connection with others is just a click away. Because of the technological mediums involved, communications can be kept secret and can get intense very quickly.

But just to be clear, we're *not* advising that everyone abandon social media, texting and email. We *are* suggesting that you be mindful of how you are utilizing your technological mediums so you can enjoy them in a way that does not detract from your relationship with each other. So the technology *itself* isn't bad. It can absolutely be used for good and in moderation, and it truly does facilitate staying connected with family and friends. In fact, it offers a whole new way to nurture your relationship. This *Facebook* post from Cindy is a great example:

"My husband amazes me...just stops by my mom's this morning to see how she is and to say hello...taking the time to care. Thanks, Ted. I love you."

You can imagine how good it felt for Cindy to write what she did and for Ted to read it wherever he was during his workday.

So… when is the last time *you* texted, emailed or FB'd your partner just to say something nice or even flirty? (Schedule confirmations don't count!) There is a PIE waiting for you in Chapter Three that will make sure your answer is "Quite recently in fact!"

Chapter Two

CoupleFlow Step Two:
Get On the Same Page

If you are like most of us and can relate to at least some degree of dissatisfaction or frustration in your relationship, you are in a position to be proactive so that your rough edges don't grow into major tears. We know that when you share a willingness to stop blaming each other (to any degree) for your frustrations and to focus on intentionally partnering as a way of life, deep and meaningful improvement can occur. It's often a matter of casting the old, underperforming aspects of the relationship aside to make room for the new and improved features. The goodwill, passion and partnership that characterized your relationship's early days can absolutely be resuscitated. But this time around, you will have a new skill

> *When you share a willingness to stop blaming each other for your frustrations and to focus on intentionally partnering as a way of life, deep and meaningful improvement can occur.*

set to rely on that allows you to energize and reinforce all of these warm, positive feelings. You'll also have systems in place to recover from the inevitable rough patches ahead.

Even couples who have been seriously struggling can transform their relationship into a strong, vibrant and enduring relationship that each partner is grateful to be a part of. We see this in our office regularly! And if that's true, then it stands to reason that couples who are on more solid footing, yet still looking to make improvements, are fully capable of doing so also.

Whichever category you identify most closely with, the key variables in either situation are *willingness* and the *proper plan*.

This chapter will allow you to confirm your willingness and get started on your plan. One common pitfall for couples seeking to improve their sexual and emotional intimacy is to go straight for the many quick-fix techniques and interventions available via the Internet and countless other media outlets. They skip over the basic foundation building that enables positive changes to gain traction and endure. We want to prevent that from happening to you in this program. So in the spirit of first things first, there are some important questions that need answers before moving into your plan of action.

Question # 1: Are We on the Same Page?

> *"My husband doesn't put his name on anything unless he is fully behind it, so I knew he was serious about doing this with me."*
> -Tracy, 40

Why This Matters:

Your *CoupleFlow* launch will be off to a strong start the moment each of you clearly confirms your willingness to participate fully. This is one area in which you cannot be too clear with each other because it relates directly to your investment in your relationship. Without a clear answer to the question posed by the title of this PIE, you would probably be better off postponing the rest of this book until you *do* have a clear answer. As confident as we are in the program we have created for you, we know this program will not work if either one of you is ambivalent about giving this an honest, good-faith effort. It all begins with the *"CoupleFlow* Program Agreement." This is a way for you to indicate that you are clearly committed to investing the focus and emotional energy that will be necessary to get the most out of this program. Knowing that your levels of commitment are in alignment exponentially increases the probability of making tangible improvements in your Living Room and Bedroom. You don't need to have everything figured out in order to say, *"I'm all in."*

Guidelines:

- In the contract that follows, you are asked to indicate your willingness to: 1. engage this program with all your best efforts, and 2. to not change course unilaterally.
- Read the statement in the contract below out loud together, then sign your name in the indicated area.

- If for any reason it is difficult to do so, let your partner know what obstacles are causing you to hesitate.

CoupleFlow Program Agreement

- *I understand that I am agreeing to work together as partners toward the goal of strengthening a mutually satisfying relationship characterized by healthy emotional and sexual intimacy.*
- *I promise to do my very best to be a good partner to you throughout this process.*
- *By signing below, I pledge my commitment to work with you in this process until we both agree that we have created a healthy, robust and proactive process of emotional and sexual connecting that we can maintain.*
- *If I have any thoughts about stopping before we finish the CoupleFlow program, I promise to share them directly with you so we can discuss them in partnership.*

_____   _____

Name   Date

_____   _____

Name   Date

Question #2: For Better and for Worse: What is it Like Being in Relationship with <u>Me</u>?

<u>Why this Matters</u>:

It's easy to look across the table and see the faults, annoying idiosyncrasies and relational deficits of the person sitting across from you. It is more difficult (and far more productive) to look within yourself to see what *you* contribute to your relationship challenges. When you do, you usually see that "Living with me isn't always a day at the beach either!" When you acknowledge how it must not always be easy to be in relationship *with you*, then you are in a position to feel empathy for your partner and to think about what you might want to change on your side of things. So keep in mind that nothing improves the circulation between your Living Room and Bedroom like clearing the air on your side of the room. However, some people find that listing their negative contributions to the relationship is uncomfortable due to fears that such admissions could be used against them by their partner. If this is a concern of yours, it may help to get some reassurance that this will not happen. Letting your partner know that you are feeling uncomfortable (and why) gives you a chance to honor your feelings and gives your partner a chance to be there for you.

Of course, there are also legitimate qualities and benefits that you bring to your relationship as well. Why is it so important to be aware of the specific ways you bring value? If you don't think you bring value, you are more likely to accept a position of lower status in your relationship, which is never a good thing. So this PIE guides you in conducting a thorough self-assessment regarding *all* that you bring to your relationship: the contributions you are proud of as well as those habits and characteristics you imagine must make life difficult for your partner.

Guidelines:

- First you will focus on the qualities you bring to your relationship under the heading, *"For Better."* consider the benefits of being in relationship with you. What do you truly feel good about contributing to your relationship? List as many qualities that you can think of.
- Next, under the heading, *"For Worse,"* focus on your own faults, annoying idiosyncrasies and all the things that you imagine do not make life easy for your partner. Make a list of these things that you do not feel good about contributing to your relationship. Here is a sample:

For Better:

1. I am a good cook. 2. I am organized. 3. I plan fun things for us to do as a couple. 4. I am warm and loving. 5. I am committed to being a good parent. 6. I get over stuff pretty quickly. 7. I am a sensitive lover.

For Worse:

1. I can be critical and irritable. 2. I can be irresponsible with spending too much money. 3. I am easily distracted. 4. I sometimes lose track of time or am late. 5. One way I get over stuff is to avoid talking about it. 6. I have less sexual desire than I used to.

- Plan a time to share these inventories with each other. Take note of the feelings that come up for you as you read your lists. (Some people experience guilt or even shame when reading their "For Worse" list). Also notice any emotions that surface as you listen to your partner, but do not comment while your partner is reading.

- When each of you has had a chance to finish reading your inventories, then also take turns giving feedback (not criticism) to each other based on what you just heard. For example, you may wonder, "So what did you think of my assessment?" Your partner might answer, "I really appreciated you owning what you did, especially spending too much. And I could make an even longer "For Better" list for you!"

- By the way, if any weighty issues cross your mind, this is *not* the time to air them. Make a note, and save them for another time. Be sure to thank your partner for joining you in completing this self-assessment with integrity.

Question # 3: What Do I Really *Like* about You?

> *"I felt really appreciated when he read his list. There were a couple of nice surprises that definitely put a smile on my face."*
> -Maggie, 52

Why This Matters:

The positive qualities that you initially saw in each other formed the basis for your attraction. As your relationship deepened, you probably found even more attractive qualities in each other. But keeping the positive thoughts and images of each other in the front of your minds is not always easy, especially when under stress or when in conflict. That is why it is essential to intentionally reconnect with all the things you genuinely appreciate and find attractive about each other. This can have a tremendous effect on the flow between your Living Room and Bedroom. Maintaining an open mind and a grateful heart throughout this PIE will help things along.

Guidelines:

- Make a list that includes all of your partner's characteristics that make him/her attractive to you. These can be personality characteristics, physical characteristics or anything you can think of. Include what attracted you to your partner in the first place, even if some of those factors are less noticeable now. Also think about what you did not know about your partner in the beginning of your relationship that you now find attractive (e.g., "You are such a great mother." "You have overcome so much adversity"). Do not worry about how long your list is, just focus on whatever is true for you.

- Finally, share your lists with each other. After each of you has shared your lists, consider the following questions for discussion:
  - Did you hear anything from your partner that was a pleasant surprise?
  - What did you find most meaningful in your partner's list of your attractive qualities? Was there anything you had hoped to hear, but did not?
  - Was there anything that was nice to hear but that you have a hard time accepting?

Chapter Three

CoupleFlow StepThree:
Let's Talk About Sex!

OK, raise your hand if you skipped right to this chapter! We completely understand if that's what you did, since this is the chapter where we are definitely going to begin turning up the heat in the Bedroom...but we'll be taking a perhaps unexpected path to get there. *"Why not just take the shortcut?"* you may ask. First of all, we know that you already have an endless supply of potentially hot sex techniques available to you. They are as close as your next Google search or your next issue of Cosmo or Men's Health. We didn't write this book simply to add another page to a very thick existing body of suggestions.

The *CoupleFlow* model you are learning is built to last. You may be encouraged to know that this model does not sacrifice pleasure in the name of durability. As you will see, the *CoupleFlow* model encourages as much fun and pleasure in the Bedroom as you like -- it allows you to appreciate what you have now and to leave plenty of room for more! We'll be showing you very clearly how to

> *The CoupleFlow model encourages as much fun and pleasure in the Bedroom as you like.*

maintain your Bedroom at a steady simmer, (where heat waves are always welcome) instead of a quick sizzle and fizzle. It begins with developing a better sense for your sexual self as well as your partner's.

SEXUAL SELF-ASSESSMENT

When is the last time you slowed down enough to consider all the various aspects of your sexuality? If you're like most people, it's probably been a while (and perhaps you never *really* have). The reason is that we usually approach our sexuality like we do so many other things: We are not motivated to slow down and carefully consider it unless there is a problem. If some kind of sexual dissatisfaction is what motivated you to read this book, then you are definitely in the right place. If you wouldn't go so far as to say you've been having problems, but you would like to *see how good things can get*, then you are *also* in the right place.

So here's your chance. Rather than an academic exercise, this is the first step to bringing your sexual intimacy into alignment with the vision you will develop in Step Four of this book. No matter where you were starting from when you began this program, *knowing your sexual self is a prerequisite for all aspects of Bedroom improvements.* Understanding your sexual preferences and turn-ons as well as your sexual hang-ups and obstacles is an absolute must. Without this refined level of sexual self-awareness, trying to improve sexual intimacy would be like building a house beginning with the interior decorating. Even the best decorator in the universe can't do much without seeing the structure of the home and getting a sense of the flow from one room to the next and of each of the resident's preferences.

The next section will guide you in developing a clear working knowledge of your sexual self. This will put you in a strong position to share your self-assessment with your partner as you prepare to welcome Sexual Abundance into your relationship.

SEXUAL ATTITUDES AND HISTORY SURVEY™

Please provide brief responses to the following:

1. The *messages* I received in my home about sexuality were:
2. The *information* I received at home about sexuality was:
3. The messages I received at school (and/or church) about sexuality was:
4. My parents' attitudes toward sexuality were :
5. My parents showed affection to each other by:
6. My parents showed affection to me by:
7. When my body started developing sexually, I felt:
8. My family reacted _____ (positively, negatively, not at all) to my developing body.
9. In my home, nudity was …
10. Were you ever touched inappropriately by an older adolescent or adult?
11. How did you feel about your sexuality growing up and what was most influential?
12. How would you describe your body image as a child compared to now?
13. Do you know how your same-sex parent felt about his/her body?
14. At what age do you remember discovering your genitals, and what do you recall?
15. How did your peers tend to view you physically and sexually? (Attractive/Unattractive? Loose? A prude? A tease?)
16. What did you learn from your childhood peers about sex and sexuality?
17. What messages did you receive about masturbation (and from whom)?
18. Describe your masturbation history up to the present.
19. How did you decide to begin having sexual experiences?

20. When you began having sexual experiences, what were the situations and what were your reactions to the experiences?

21. How did you feel about yourself after becoming sexually active?

22. Was there ever anything you were ashamed of or too embarrassed to tell anyone as a child/adolescent/young adult?

23. How do you currently feel about your sexuality? Does it differ from how you would like to feel?

Finishing Instructions:

Now that you have taken your own sexual inventory, it is time to consolidate your responses into two responses to the questions below that address your *past's* influence on your *present* (wait to share your responses until instructed to do so in the upcoming "Your Turn" Section).

1. What would you say have been some of the most influential factors that have promoted a *healthy* sense of your sexual self?

2. Which factors represent unwanted sexual baggage and have *negatively* impacted your sexual self?

SEXUAL PREFERENCES SURVEY™

Rate the following activities and preferences according to this scale:

1 = NOT for me

2 = Not one of my favorites

3 = Would LIKE to like it/try it -- let's talk!

4 = Definitely like it

5 = Can't get enough!

_____ Me initiating sensual/sexual affection

_____ You initiating sensual/sexual affection

_____ Dressing for the occasion (lingerie, etc.)

_____ Cuddling

_____ Kissing (lips)

_____ Kissing (open mouth/ "making out")

_____ Body caressing

_____ Breast caressing

_____ Nipple caressing/kissing

_____ Taking bath together

_____ Taking shower together

_____ Giving sexual touch

_____ Receiving sexual touch

Pace of sexual touch:

_____Fast/hard

_____Slow/soft

_____ Giving oral sex

_____ Receiving oral sex

_____ Sexual intercourse

Pace of intercourse:

_____Fast/aggressive

_____Slow/gentle

_____Experimenting with different positions

_____ Using sexual toys/vibrator

_____Quickies

_____Marathons

_____ Anal stimulation (external)

_____ Anal stimulation (internal)

_____Sexual activity in places other than bedroom

_____ Role playing

_____ Sharing fantasies

Communicating during sexual activity:

_____Saying what feels good

_____Talking "sexy" (as you define it)

_____Talking "dirty" (as you define it)

_____Physical redirection (e.g., moving each other's hands)

_____ *Anything(s) not on this list*

_____

• •

Now go back and rate what you think *your partner* would say for each of the above activities. When you are finished, jot down some brief responses to the following:

- Which of the above activities would you prefer *more* of?

- Which of the above have you been *hesitant (or embarrassed) to discuss?*

- Which of the above activities that you rated "2" or above do you think have the potential to be even *more enjoyable?* What might help them to BE more enjoyable?

- Finally, are you aware of any factors affecting your sexual enjoyment that you would like to discuss? It could be how you prefer to be approached, how you begin your sexual times together, the time of day that you typically get together sexually, hygiene issues, sexual functioning, weight, body image, health, etc. These can be challenging issues to raise, but the next section will help you do so with sensitivity and compassion.

SHARING SEXUAL REALITIES

One of our new, favorite radio talk show hosts, Elaina McMillan of WKRP's *Naked Talk Radio*, is known for her catchphrase, "So are you ready to *get naked*?" It isn't a cue to strip down, but rather an invitation to reveal something personal that may be difficult because of longstanding feelings of embarrassment or awkwardness around sexuality. Even people who consider themselves comfortable discussing sexuality in frank terms may still have some areas that aren't *quite* as easy to discuss as others.

Keep all of this in mind and give yourself plenty of room to feel however you feel as you complete the next exercise: sharing the results of your self-assessments with each other. After reading through the upcoming "Your Turn" section, you will walk each other through your responses. Take time to expand on any of your own responses or to ask questions of each other. A general rule of thumb is that it's always acceptable to say, "This is something I'd like to know/talk more about" and to then leave the door open to future discussions around sexual matters. As you let each other in, perhaps in some ways that you ordinarily would not think to do, keep in mind that this can be a very vulnerable process (even if you're not feeling anxious). Because of this, a non-judgmental atmosphere is essential.

The process of sharing with each other can open up many new frontiers of possibility and understanding. For example, Jonathan had long been aware of Candace's resistance to receiving oral sex. Dating back to their early sexual encounters, it had been the subject of many conflicts, with Jonathan pleading with Candace to "Just *try* it!" Candace would say she thought it was "gross" and ask him why he couldn't just be happy with the things she *did* like to do sexually. She had become so upset the last time he brought it up that Jonathan hadn't even mentioned it in the two years since. So, Jonathan was not surprised to hear that Candace rated "Receiving oral sex" a "2" ("Not one of my favorites"). However, he was somewhat *shocked* that she *also* listed it as something she thought *could be* more enjoyable. She told Jonathan that over the years she had read a couple books on female sexuality and even talked with a few girlfriends about what they like most about sex. She told Jonathan she realized she might be missing out on something that plenty of other women seemed to really enjoy with their husbands and she wondered if there might be a way for her to see if she could too. However, she also said she had been afraid to tell him all this for fear that he would make it his issue and try to speed up her process. She asked him to please give her the space she would need to explore her comfort with this activity.

Jonathan was very compassionate to Candace, telling her how much he appreciated her letting him in. He apologized for putting pressure on her in the past and reassured her that he'd give her all the room in the world. He asked her to let him know how he could help her feel comfortable. She said she couldn't think of anything specific right then, but she did ask him to be patient. To her pleasant

> *Without even touching physically, they enhanced their sexual connection.*

surprise, Jonathan replied, "It's your body and your comfort. Sure, I'd like to see how much fun we could have with it, but this one is really about you. I'll meet you wherever you're at." She had never heard Jonathan speak so sensitively about this topic and was encouraged that they could talk about it in frank terms without it turning into a huge fight. In this one exchange they had engineered their *CoupleFlow* in a freshly empowered direction. Without even touching physically, they enhanced their sexual connection, and through their honest sharing with each other they added another layer of emotional intimacy.

Similarly, Mike and Danielle, married for 15 years, came away from this PIE with vastly enhanced understandings of each other's sexual realities, and a stronger Living Room to Bedroom connection. When Danielle heard from Mike how shamed he had been by his ex-fiancé for his occasional erectile dysfunction and premature ejaculation, she understood why it was so difficult for him to initiate sex with her. This had long been a big source of hurt and confusion for Danielle, as she seriously questioned his attraction to her. It turned out that Mike had been so shamed in this earlier relationship that he had felt too embarrassed to share it with Danielle, until now. She couldn't thank him enough for trusting her with something so laden with vulnerability, and also for giving her important background information that allowed her to stop doubting herself and to be more compassionate toward him.

In the same way, when Mike heard from Danielle how her father would make comments about women who "don't take care of themselves," he understood more about why Danielle seemed so hard on herself regarding her body and appearance. When they shared the results of their *Sexual Preferences Survey*, they realized that they had very similar ideas about what they would like to experiment with and enjoy more of (sex toys, new positions, bathing together). They resolved not to let *another* 15 years go by without talking openly and honestly about their sexual realities!

YOUR TURN

So now it's your turn to let each other in on your responses to the *Sexual Attitudes and History* questionnaire and the *Sexual Preferences Scale*. We suggest that you start by sharing your responses to the questions at the end of each of these self-assessments. Then you can go back and review specific items. If openly discussing your sexuality is difficult for you due to embarrassment, anxiety or awkwardness, definitely let your partner know. Many people also

> *Making clear requests about sexual preferences works best ... and it doesn't make what you receive any less meaningful.*

struggle with this part due to an expectation or hope that their partner would *just know* these things by now. As one woman put it, "I shouldn't need to gift wrap all of my preferences and give them to him, just so he can give the box right back to me." We say that whether it's gifts of jewelry, clothing, *or* sexual pleasure, leaving it to chance may work out sometimes, but making clear requests works *a lot* more often and it doesn't make what you receive any less meaningful.

A word of advice before you share your responses... we devoted the majority of an entire chapter (*"Protect to Connect"*) to healthy boundaries because they are essential for helping conversations like this to feel safe. So, now is a great time to make sure your boundaries are working for you in both directions: When you listen, know that everything you are hearing is about your partner, even when it involves you. When you share, you are sharing *your* perspective, *your* reality, simply to let your partner know *your* truth. Honest, respectful dialogue about sexuality allows you to take charge of your *CoupleFlow* and to have fun while you're doing it.

Something you'll notice at the end of the physical PIEs that is designed to lead to some honest dialogue is a rating box. It will take just a moment to rate each of the physical PIEs (on scale of 1-5), but these numbers won't speak for themselves. To get the most out of these ratings, explain *why* you rated the PIE the way you did. For example, let each other know what your "3" means (and how it could move up to a 4 or 5). Be careful not to blame each other for any low-rated PIEs -- you're rating the PIE and your unique experience of it, *not* each other. The ratings give you a chance to very efficiently highlight what you like and better understand if and how you could enjoy the activity even more.

Performance is for Athletes and Actors, not Lovers

"Come in today, perform tonight!" screams the tagline from a radio ad for a popular male medical clinic. *"Never Let Your Performance Disappoint Her Again!"* responds the print ad from a competitor. And not to be outdone, yet another male clinic's marketing campaign offers an easy way to tell if you'll be celebrating a certain romantic holiday: *"Valentine's Day is for Lovers...Unless You Have Performance Issues!"* These ads are consistent with our cultural norms around sex as an activity to be evaluated, measured and judged. Though men may experience more pressure to "perform" due to the more obvious indicator of their sexual arousal and the necessity of an

> *When you are feeling really good about your Bedroom, it is not because every sexual experience is perfectly scripted and flawlessly executed.*

erection for intercourse, women are not immune from performance pressure -- not with the typical Hollywood sex scene lasting about 45 seconds and ending in her climactic shrieks. And certainly not with the proliferation of online porn where she is constantly portrayed as insatiable and up for anything at anytime, anywhere. She knows *exactly* what to do to bring her man to new sexual heights *every time* and she does it *on demand*.

When sex is approached with pre-conceived notions about how one or both partners *should* respond, the odds of the desired response drop dramatically. Not only that, you are likely to miss the all-important emotional and spiritual bonding power of your sexual time. A common example is when a couple prioritizes simultaneous orgasms.

> *A common example is when a couple prioritizes simultaneous orgasms.*

They typically end up more focused on crossing this finish line together than on everything that takes place in advance of it. We have counseled several couples who were quite

~ 119 ~

frustrated with their inability to consistently reach this goal. They were convinced that they had Bedroom problems although everything else seemed to be wonderful! When you are really feeling good about your Bedroom, it is not because every sexual experience is perfectly scripted and flawlessly executed. On the contrary, *CoupleFlow* in the Bedroom is characterized by the freedom and novelty of NOT knowing exactly what will happen and how things will unfold. As you will see in the following section, your ability to make real-time adjustments within an atmosphere of realistic expectations has more to do with Bedroom bliss than any sexual scorecard could ever measure.

Managing Expectations, Making Adjustments

Great sex within Sexual Abundance means leaving a lot of room for your sexual experiences to vary. If you expect that you and your partner are going to reach newfound heights of arousal every time you get together, you're setting yourself up for disappointment. In fact, in a study by Drs. Barry and Emily McCarthy, it was revealed that only 40-50% of the time do *both* partners walk away from a sexual experience saying it was "very good" for each of them. Of these very good experiences, only 5-10% rate "special." (By the way, only

> *CoupleFlow in the Bedroom is characterized by the freedom and novelty of NOT knowing exactly what will happen and how things will unfold.*

couples who said they were *satisfied with their sex life* were included in this study!) So what often ends up happening is that many couples have completely normal variability in the quality of their sexual experiences, but feel as if they are falling short. They place their Bedroom under an unnecessarily glaring spotlight, and experience a kind of self-fulfilling prophecy.

Normal variability in the Bedroom yields many opportunities to partner together and make real-time adjustments as you go along in any given sexual encounter. This is so important because you can have many different reactions and go in several different directions in response to the same conditions. Consider the condition of John's erection losing strength during intercourse:

Scenario 1: John stops and says, "Well, I guess it's not gonna happen tonight." He rolls over onto his side and stares off into space, feeling utterly frustrated, helpless and inadequate. His wife, Melinda, is afraid to suggest anything else because she senses that John is too fragile in the moment to hear anything from her. She caresses John's shoulder, as if to say, "It's OK," but removes her hand when she feels him tensing up. Another layer of anxiety builds in anticipation of the next time.

Scenario 2: John slows down and says, "Well I guess Mr. Happy isn't playing along tonight. Wanna try something else?" Melinda does not want their sexual experience to end just because John lost his erection, so she enthusiastically replies, "Absolutely. Do you want me to give him some special attention?" John appreciates how Melinda is just rolling with it, and says, "Actually, let's give him a little break. I was thinking more along the lines of giving *you* some special attention." Instead of the end of the line, this was merely the middle of a very pleasurable, very connecting, very warm and very fun time of enjoying each other.

Another example comes courtesy of Helen's elusive orgasm:

Scenario 1: After 30 minutes of oral and manual stimulation and intercourse, Helen still hasn't reached orgasm. Her frustration mounting, she says, "OK -- stop. That's not working. You're not doing it right. Just forget it, let's try me on top again." Frank is frustrated by now also, and feels like he is letting Helen down because no matter what he tries, he just can't bring her to orgasm.

"OK, but I'm doing everything I can!" he blurts out. "I know, but every time I get close, you change something. C'mon stop talking." Three position changes later, it became clear that there would be no "O" for Helen that night, only disappointment that they couldn't get it right. Neither could say they were looking forward to the next time.

Scenario 2: After 30 minutes of oral and manual stimulation and intercourse, Helen still hasn't reached orgasm. She understands that this happens sometimes and she realizes that Frank has been very attentive to her while waiting to have his own orgasm. "Honey, if you're ready, go ahead," Helen offers. "You sure?" asks Frank. "Yes, but I still might not be through with you, OK?" Frank did not need any time to think through his response: *"Deal!"* Frank did not feel guilty or inadequate because he knew it wasn't his *job* to make Helen orgasm. He also trusted that she was enjoying their time, *even if it didn't result in orgasm.* After Frank had his moment, Helen asked Frank to kiss her breasts and manually stimulate her. As much as she relished the waves of pleasure, there would be no "O" for Helen that night. But that's not what she nor Frank would remember most. The memory of their shared passion and connectedness fueled their anticipation for the next time. They couldn't wait.

What is It Like *in the Bedroom* with Me?

Why This Matters:

Whether you have a nagging insecurity, a mild curiosity, or even if it's never crossed your mind, it can be very Bedroom-positive to consider how your partner experiences you sexually. It is natural to be more aware of ways in which you wish your partner was more this or less that in the Bedroom. Less natural and more vulnerable is looking at what *you* contribute. This PIE asks you to take an honest look at yourself and to give and receive feedback from your partner. If you are feeling uneasy right now just contemplating this exercise, let your partner know. Reassure each other that this is a time for sensitivity, not critique.

Guidelines:

Reflect on the following questions and share you responses with your partner:

1. What do you believe you contribute *in a positive way* to your Bedroom atmosphere and experience? For example, how do you keep things interesting? How are you proactive in ways that get the two of you together in the first place and allow for mutually enjoyable encounters? How are you sensitive to your partner's Bedroom experience?

2. What do you believe you contribute to your Bedroom that may be *challenging or inhibiting* for your partner? Are there areas that are difficult for you or that you are insecure about? (initiating, giving or receiving pleasure, weight or other physical concerns, etc.) What do you think (or fear) your partner would say?

3. What do you appreciate about your partner's contributions to your Bedroom atmosphere and experience?

4. If there is one thing you might ask you partner to be more aware of regarding your Bedroom experience, what would it be?

Just the Backs

Why This Matters:

This PIE is designed to allow you to enjoy the new type of touch you are learning in a specific way that focuses on your back. Many people have experience in giving and receiving a back *massage*. Here, you are asked to experiment with a lighter type of touch than a traditional massage in order to elevate the intimacy potential. Rather than simply relieving muscle tension, gently caressing the back in this experience will allow each of you to feel closely connected through touch. There is much surface area to cover on the back, and you are encouraged to explore the sensual pleasure potential that this area holds. You will be expanding your capacity to slow things down and to appreciate a broad range of sensual pleasure. The environment is set up to be free of demand or expectations of any kind. The emphasis is on experimenting with a new type of touch within the context of the structure provided in the instructions below.

Guidelines:

- This experience can occur wherever you think would be comfortable. You will take turns caressing and being caressed on your backs (this includes everything from the back of your head and arms down to your hips).
- The receiver can then remove his/her shirt and find a comfortable position while lying face-down.
- As the caresser, let your enjoyment of your partner's body guide your touch. You can assume that your partner is enjoying the touch unless s/he redirects you. You can be

aware of the nuances of your partner's back, and can appreciate being trusted with your partner's vulnerability.

- As the receiver, you can notice how your partner's touch feels different as it moves from one area to another. You might also appreciate the careful attention that your partner is demonstrating. You will redirect your partner anytime you realize that you would prefer a different type of touch. Whenever it occurs to either of you that you have had enough time caressing or being caressed, this should be expressed so you can switch roles (receiver becomes caresser, caresser becomes receiver).

- Arousal is not the main goal for this PIE or any others, meaning you are not setting out to see how intense your arousal can get. The goal is simply to be present with each other and to be aware of everything that you are experiencing. However, if you do notice yourself becoming aroused during any of these PIEs, feel free to enjoy it!

Talk about it:

- What did you enjoy the most? Did you encounter any barriers? If so, would you make any modifications?
- What emotions *were* you aware of? What are your feelings toward your partner *now*?

Rate it:_____

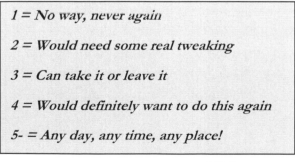

1 = No way, never again

2 = Would need some real tweaking

3 = Can take it or leave it

4 = Would definitely want to do this again

5- = Any day, any time, any place!

Kiss Me!

Why This Matters:

Does it seem like eternity ago when you used to kiss each other all the time? If so, you are not alone. It is quite common for kissing to decline in frequency and enjoyment over time. A related pattern can develop where kissing playing a mere signaling role, indicating that someone wants to have sex. There may be a gender correlation as well, namely that many women really miss the pleasure of kissing just for the sake of kissing. However, some women hesitate to initiate kissing when they think that it might send the message that she also wants to be sexual -- but all she really wants is to plant a big one on him or even just make out! One of the reasons kissing was so enjoyable during early courtship was that you knew kissing was the *main event*, so you were able to enjoy kissing on its own. You were able to enjoy kissing passionately, embracing it for its uniquely connecting pleasure. Now is the time for you to claim (or reclaim) the pleasure of kissing.

Kissing can be one of, if not *the* most intimate ways of connecting with each other. Why? Not only are the lips one of the most sensitive areas to touch on our entire bodies, they're surrounded by all of our other windows of sensory input: sight, smell, hearing, taste. When you bring together these most sensitive parts, it is a true act of trust and intimacy. This may explain why some say they see fireworks during a kiss! This PIE also provides another opportunity to share your preferences directly with your partner. There really is no right or wrong way to kiss because of the wide range of different preferences. An openness to share with and learn from each other will continue to build trust and intimacy in your relationship. Finally, remember that the spirit of this PIE is fun, open, and experimenting. So let yourselves laugh, try kissing in some new ways, and if it feels like you are rewinding the hands of time, then so be it.

Guidelines:

- This experience can occur wherever you think you would be most comfortable. You will be taking turns leading the kissing and being kissed. (It may go without saying, but everyone prefers a freshly brushed, minty mouth).
- Decide who wants to be kissed first and who will lead first.
- As the one *leading the kissing*, show your partner the kind(s) of kissing you enjoy most.
- Experiment with any new ways of kissing you think might be fun. Consider kissing in areas other than the lips, such as the neck, ears, cheeks, or hair if this is enjoyable.
- As the person *being led* in the kissing, you can simply follow your partner's lead, unless you are being led in a way that is not enjoyable or comfortable for you. If this occurs, then share your preference with your partner. (e.g., "Could you keep going with a little less tongue?" or "This is amazing, but my neck is so ticklish -- could you please go back to kissing my lips?")
- When you have had enough time, switch roles so that you each get a turn leading.
- If applicable, discuss any obstacles to kissing you are aware of and how you might change things to work around them.

Talk about it:

- What did you enjoy the most?
- What did you learn about how your partner prefers kissing?
- What feelings were you aware of? What are your feelings toward your partner now?
- Would you like to do more kissing in the future?

Rate it:_____

1 = No way, never again
2 = Would need some real tweaking
3 = Can take it or leave it
4 = Would definitely want to do this again
5 = Any day, any time, any place!

THE FICKLE FLAME OF SEXUAL DESIRE

It's difficult to find anything that is both as predictable *and* unpredictable as sexual desire. First, let's begin with the predictable factors that absolutely positively affect sexual desire:

Positive regard for your partner*:* This one may seem as if it goes without saying, but it's so key to the *CoupleFlow* model and Sexual Abundance. We would go so far as to say that foreplay really begins in the Living Room, where a consistently warm connection with each other keeps the Bedroom door propped open.

Sexual enjoyment*:* Human nature is to feel drawn toward activities that have been enjoyable before. If you had a great workout this morning, chances are you'll be positively anticipating tomorrow's workout. If you had a great meal at a new restaurant, we bet you'll be back again soon. Had a passionate, toe-curling Bedroom encounter recently? That's *exactly* what will keep you coming back for more. This is why it is so important to have excellent Bedroom communication, so you know what lets each other's good times roll!

Physical health*:* You may not be thinking in terms of your sex drive when you're straining to complete those last few crunches, but the way you care for your body absolutely intersects with your libido. If you have noticed that when you feel good about yourself physically, you feel more connected to your sexuality, then you have a lot of company. A healthy diet, regular exercise and adequate rest may not sound sexy, but they go a long way toward *feeling* sexy.

Hormone levels: One of the first things we insist on when a client complains of low desire is to get a complete hormone panel assessment. The hormones most related to sexual desire and arousal are testosterone (for men *and* women) as well as estrogen and progesterone (for women). The fact is, no matter how strong your Living Room flow is, or how much you typically enjoy your Bedroom encounters with your partner, if your hormone levels are abnormal, your desire and responsiveness will *absolutely* be affected. Here's a quick reference guide:

Estrogen: Estrogen helps to regulate the menstrual cycle, but as menopause approaches, estrogen levels begin falling sharply. Other endocrine system factors can also cause estrogen levels to fall below normal levels in otherwise healthy women of any age, causing a major drag on your libido. Vaginal dryness is a common symptom which makes intercourse painful.

Testosterone: Testosterone goes hand in hand with being a man, but women naturally produce testosterone also. Research indicates a clear correlation between abnormally low testosterone levels and low sexual desire for both genders. Testosterone levels begin to fall off gradually during a man's thirties while women can expect a similar decline during menopause. So at a certain age, you may need to allow for some adjustments in the Bedroom due to lower testosterone levels. For example, men may require more direct genital stimulation to achieve and maintain an erection while women may benefit from use of personal lubricant. If your sexual responsiveness becomes less predictable less than during younger years, you also can adjust by redefining what makes for a successful Bedroom experience (not orgasm dependent, but flexible enough to follow your pleasure in various directions).

Considering Hormone Replacement Therapy

There's an important distinction to be made between normal hormone decline that does not cause symptoms that significantly inhibit sexual desire and arousal and abnormally low hormone levels which clearly interfere with sexual satisfaction. If you experience noticeable changes in sexual desire or responsiveness or if you have been living with these issues for some time, you should consult your medical doctor to see if any of the following Hormone Replacement Therapy options are appropriate for you:

Estrogen therapy: Taking estrogen hormone therapy can help relieve symptoms of low estrogen levels, including vaginal dryness. For many women, estrogen therapy can make sex more comfortable and enjoyable. However, since estrogen therapy has been associated with an increased risk of endometrial cancer, it is recommended that women with an intact uterus take progesterone along with estrogen, to reduce this risk.

Topical estrogen: Another way to deliver estrogen to your body is through vaginal estrogen creams. These creams are thought to help increase vaginal lubrication and sexual arousal in postmenopausal women.

Testosterone therapy: Many studies have looked at using testosterone supplementation to help improve sexual desire in men and women with sexual dysfunction. Researchers have found that testosterone therapy may improve sexual desire in postmenopausal women who have problems with sex drive and sexual satisfaction as well as with men who notice problematic sexual functioning, including significantly decreased sexual desire. Consult your medical doctor to see if your bioavailable ("free") testosterone should be tested.

Because these treatments carry risks, fully discuss the pros and cons of each option with your doctor. In some cases, simple lifestyle changes, such as stress management and getting adequate sleep and exercise, may restore sexual desire without the risks of hormonal therapies.

While the factors listed above have predictable influences on sexual desire, it is important to remember that desire sometimes varies *without* any clear explanation. We're not talking about a pronounced pattern of low desire, but those occasional patches when you or your partner just aren't feeling in the mood. When your *CoupleFlow* is consistently strong, you will be able to absorb these variations in desire.

Also important to keep in mind is that while it may be highly coveted, *free-floating desire* is NOT a prerequisite for a robust and mutually satisfying sex life. Many people report an absence of this kind of desire, yet they *also* report enjoying their sexual times a great deal. They understand that instead

> *When your CoupleFlow is consistently strong, you will be able to absorb variations in desire.*

of relying on something that isn't there to lead them to the Bedroom, they need to be proactive. They realize they need to *decide* to be available sexually. They find this approach highly rewarding because it allows them to enjoy all the benefits of Sexual Abundance regardless of whether they actually feel sexual in *advance* of any given Bedroom encounter. Their consistently enjoyable Bedroom times provide a reference point they come to trust, such that "even if I'm not feeling sexual desire, when I set my intentions in the direction of a positive sexual experience, I'm usually glad I did." The next PIE is a natural follow-up to the topic of desire, specifically how that desire (or lack thereof) translates into you and your partner actually getting together in the Bedroom.

Sexual Frequency: What's the Magic Number?

> *"This was the first discussion on this topic I can remember feeling like we were on the same side."*
> *–Annie, 47*

Why This Matters:

Whenever the topic of sexual frequency comes up during one of our seminars, people always want to know one thing…what's normal? In other words, how often is everyone *else* doing it? Sure, we could cite survey research and say that statistically speaking, couples in your age bracket are sexual 2.37 times per week. Or 1.12 times. Or 3.65 times. Is that really helpful? It's probably even less helpful when you consider that those studies only quantify rates of *intercourse*, ignoring the many other ways of enjoying highly pleasurable and connecting sensual/sexual activities.

We believe that a more holistic assessment of your Bedroom connection, one that takes into account the various ways that you enjoy each other in addition to intercourse, is most advantageous. We also think it is far more helpful for you to know the frequency of such encounters that works best for *your* relationship. Finally, it is also best to think of that frequency in terms of a *range* instead of a specific number. This way, you leave yourselves room to adapt to the inevitable conditions that get in the way (illness, business travel, menstrual cycle) as well as the conditions that *pave* the way (vacations together!) Your ability to talk directly about what frequency of any given activity works best for you (as you are open to hearing your partner's perspective) is a necessary component of sexual abundance.

Guidelines: Here is a five-step plan to increase the likelihood that you and your partner will be on the same wonderful page in the Bedroom.

1. ***Come up with your Magic Number.*** When considering sexual intimacy, what would each of you say is a frequency that you could be *minimally happy with* on a typical week or month? Now how about a different number that would be *on the high side?* In other words, this is the number that you would consider to be a great week/month in the Bedroom, but anything higher would likely wear you out. If your partner's numbers are identical to your own, there's not much left to discuss – have fun! But if not, as is very often the case, it's time to dialogue about a range you both could be at least OK with. Be sure to discuss intercourse and where it fits within your range (e.g. "2-3 Bedroom times per week, at least one of which is intercourse").

2. ***Protect your number.*** Once you come up with that range, you are now in the business of protecting those times to enjoy yourselves. That means communicating clearly about *when* the next time will be. Some couples have standing dates, or at least standing preferred times (e.g. Friday night and Sunday morning). For others it works well to set new dates each week. Regardless, you can be certain that many things will compete for the time you have set aside. Now is a great opportunity to discuss how you will handle scheduling challenges and to be clear on your preferred times, negotiating differences as necessary.

3. ***Leave room for more.*** As much as we believe in protecting dates and times for sexual intimacy, we know that spontaneity and flexible thinking can do wonders for your Bedroom. So if your next planned date is for Friday night and you are really in the mood on Thursday, there's nothing wrong with letting your partner know (as long as you understand that s/he may not be feeling as spontaneous as you are). We know of one couple whose standing Sunday afternoon date vanished when their children stopped napping. Before too long, they found themselves enjoying each other before the kids woke up in the morning. Neither considered themselves "morning people," but then again, they never knew the pre-dawn hours could be so much fun!

4. ***Don't (negatively) assume.*** Once you have your next time planned, do not look for indicators that your partner may be changing his/her mind. One couple's recent example in this department reads like a comedy of errors as they fell into the trap of making negative assumptions without seeking accurate information ... As Sandra tells it:

"A couple days ago, we made a date to have some fun together on Tuesday night after we got the kids to sleep. So Tuesday night rolls around, and I'm done with my part of the kids' bedtime routine first, so I go out on the couch to wait for Tim and I leaf through a magazine as I do. A few minutes later Tim walks through the room, sees me reading and decides to take the dog out for a little walk. While he's gone, I decide to hop over to the computer to check email, which is where he sees me when he walks back inside. So he flops on the couch and turns SportsCenter on. So I figure I might as well get cleaned up and go to bed. Which I do. By myself. Unhappily. The next morning I'm in the bathroom getting ready for work and he says, "So I guess you weren't up for anything last night." I was stunned!

'Me?' I asked. 'I thought you were the one who wasn't up for anything. You seemed more interested in the dog and SportsCenter than in me!' And he says, 'But I thought you were more interested in your magazine and email than in me. Then when you went to bed I assumed I was right.' We realized we each totally misread the situation and each of us locked in the misunderstanding by remaining silent. At least this gave us a chance to discuss how not to let that happen again."*

5. ***Whoever needs to change plans becomes responsible for rescheduling.*** Sometimes life legitimately gets in the way of even the most well-intentioned plans. If *you* need to cancel, it works best to let your partner know *why* you will not be available (e.g. feeling ill, work situation running late, etc.) and *when* you would suggest rescheduling. Then make sure you do everything you can to make your rescheduled date happen. If it's more of a mutual lack of availability, (You jointly decide to stay at the party a couple hours longer.) then it's a great chance for either of you to take the lead on establishing your rain-check date.

Hopefully, talking through this plan yields an additional layer of strength for your coupleship. If you get stuck and you're still stuck after several tries, you may need the help of a Certified Sex Therapist, especially if sexual frequency is a chronic source of conflict. And even if you are very happy with your conversation, please understand that sexual frequency preferences can vary widely over time, so revisiting this topic periodically will serve you well by keeping you up to date with each other. The following PIE can be a great way to keep you consistently within the range that you established in the Magic Number PIE. It also will help you to evaluate the drain (or risk) that technology places on your relationship.

Siri Says So!

> *"I couldn't wait for my phone to buzz so I could see what he would text back to me... and so I could try to make him blush at the office when I replied!"*
> *-Gwen, 42*

Why This Matters:

This PIE is an opportunity to decide how you can intentionally use technology to strengthen your relationship and have more fun even when you're not together. Instead of blaming technology for its distractions, you can make sure you're using it to your full advantage.

Guidelines:

Part I: Make a list of all the forms of technology you use, being as specific as possible. For example, instead of saying "Social Media sites," list each one that you actually belong to. Then place the number of hours or minutes you typically spend engaged in each one next to each item (Do not include work emails read at work, but do include any you handle from home.) Finally, place a star next to any of the items whose frequency you would like to reduce because you realize they may be taking too much of your time, energy or focus. When you are done, take a moment to share your lists with each other. Be sure to let each other know the areas where you are committed to reducing tech time. Also let each other know if you would like your partner to consider reducing tech time in any area (or if s/he forgot to list a specific technology). Here is an example:

- Email: 5hrs/wk (30-60 min/day = work emails)
- Texting: 5-10 min/day
- Facebook*: 30 - 45 min/day (usually before bed)
- Twitter: 20 min/day
- Video games*: 1hour/day
- Skype/FaceTime: 1 hour/week (with sister and cousins)
- TV*: 1.5 hours/day
- Internet surfing (via computer or phone): 30 minutes/day

Part II:

- Pick a technological medium that you can (or already) use to communicate with each other. It could be texting, emailing, FB'ing, skywriting, *whatever*, as long as you can both use it every day.
- Pick a start date, then send *one message per day* through your chosen medium to your partner for the next two weeks. This could be a flirty text or email telling your partner your plans for him/her the next time you are together or it could be a sweet, thoughtful message of appreciation or support or encouragement. The only criteria are that the communications are positive, genuine and consistent for the next two weeks.
- At the two week mark,, discuss what you've noticed from your new tech-enhanced intimacy. Is this something you want to keep going?

PORN IN THE BEDROOM: AT YOUR OWN RISK

The issue around pornography's influence on sexuality has never been more important to address than it is today, simply because pornography has never been more integrated and relevant in our culture. Our purpose here is not to assess it from a moral perspective but to ask, *"What are porn's practical implications for relationships?"* First of all, we must acknowledge the main reason for using porn -- to increase pleasurable sexual stimulation and intensity. And the fact is, few products deliver on what they promise the way porn does. So for something that so consistently produces its desired results, the next question becomes, *"Is it worth it?"* We believe you should seriously consider this question if you or and/or your partner use porn individually or view it together to enhance your Bedroom experience.

On the upside, viewing online pornography can provide a quick and convenient means to a pleasurable end. Some people can use porn in moderation, without hiding it from their spouse and without obvious detrimental effects on their relationship. In our experience this group represents the minority. Sometimes couples look to porn to spice things up in the Bedroom. When viewed together, it can help couples to discuss their sexual preferences and experiment with what they see[9].

However easy to access and ubiquitous it may be, it *is* a potentially addictive process for about 5-10% of users[10]. It tends to hook at-risk people hard and fast, leading them far past their originally intended boundaries. Like other addictions, people usually don't

---

[9] Some instructional videos (e.g. Sinclair Institute) feature real couples in committed relationships discussing their Bedrooms and demonstrating different forms of sexual expression. These differ from traditional pornography's often unrealistic, male-oriented portrayals of sexuality. If you and your spouse are looking for graphically demonstrated instruction, we would recommend these types of instructional videos as opposed to porn.
[10] www.Familysafemedia.com

know they are at-risk until they are already hooked. We have seen many people lose their careers and families and incur legal consequences because of an unmanageable relationship with porn. This was not typically the case before the early 1990's when it took at least *some* effort to purchase a magazine or video, not to mention the risk of embarrassment if witnessed doing so. Not only did the Internet make porn infinitely more accessible, affordable and anonymous, it also delivered the product in a way that was far more stimulating than any magazine or video. In fact, Dr. Patrick Carnes refers to online porn's level of intensity as "stimulation beyond the original design" of the human brain. On brain scans, online porn lights up the reward centers of the brain in a similar fashion to crack cocaine.

But let's say you're in the 90%-95% (which may be a conservative estimate) that will not develop a full-blown porn addiction. No problem, right? Well…there could be some complicating factors. First of all, on the male side of things, we are seeing a sharp increase in the number of men who struggle with Erectile Dysfunction, Delayed Orgasm and low desire who are otherwise healthy and relatively happy in their relationships. How is this

> *"Porn is the equivalent of professional wrestling: phony and superficial. It's like subsisting on a junk-food diet of Gummi bears and Gatorade when you could be having a gourmet meal."*
> -Ian Kerner, founder of *"Good in Bed"* website

possible, especially if porn is such a sure-fire turn-on? The answer lies in the seat of desire and arousal, the brain. With unprecedented levels of dopamine, oxytocin and vasoporin flooding his neuronal networks, his synapses begin to suffer burnout. His brain thereby becomes so conditioned by the sexual intensity that online porn provides, that partner sex does not yield enough of the above neurotransmitters to create positive conditions for sexual response. Simply stated, he is not nearly as responsive to the real thing as he once was.

Another porn-related trend is a growing dependence on mental imagery and scenes from porn use into partner sex in order to become aroused. Most partners are not exactly thrilled by this. The good news is that after about 30 days of abstaining from masturbating to porn, a resumption of normal functioning is possible. For some though, the abstaining is not so simple, as it becomes apparent that a level of compulsion has developed[11].

There is also the complicating factor of how porn use affects perceptions of sexually normative behaviors and sexual expectations. We hear story after story about requests from one partner to another to engage in sexual behaviors viewed online. Sometimes, the partner is willing and both enjoy the experience, but other times, the request is perceived as offensive or uncomfortable. In other instances, there is no request because one partner spontaneously introduces the behavior.

For example, Megan began to notice that her husband, Rick, was becoming rougher and using coarse language during sex that she'd never heard him use before. In the past she had appreciated how tuned into her he seemed during sex, but recently it seemed like his mind was somewhere else. When she asked him about the changes she was noticing, he told her he "just wanted to shake things up a little bit." Megan told him she was all for variety but that she was uncomfortable with his distance and language. A few weeks later while they were engaged in some passionate foreplay, Rick attempted anal sex with Megan without any discussion. This activity had never been part of their sex life and Megan was shocked. "What do you think you're doing?!" she exclaimed. That seemed to snap Rick out of his trance. "I just thought it might be fun to try something different, but I guess you aren't up for

---

[11] Wondering if you or your partner has crossed the line into porn addiction? We can help you arrive at an accurate answer and direct you toward help if necessary: www.drsbercaw.com

that," he replied. "No, I'm definitely *not* and I want to know what has gotten into you lately. Sex used to be so fun and I always felt so close to you. But now you're starting to scare me."

Eventually, Rick told Megan that he'd been doing some "online research" about sexuality and he had been drawn toward certain porn sites. Megan told him how surprised she was and that she much preferred that they discuss their sex life together as partners instead of secretly developing sexual agendas. She also let him know that she was hurt and concerned that he could so easily objectify her and she asserted that she was not okay with him continuing to visit porn sites. It wasn't easy for Rick, but he did hear Megan and after several starts and stops he was able to turn away from his attraction to porn's intensity. As he gradually moved back in the direction of his and Megan's very real sexual intimacy, he was able to appreciate that there was some nice sexual intensity there also, but with the benefit of feeling genuinely connected to his wife.

Thankfully, Rick's relationship with porn had not reached the level of active addiction, but many others are not so fortunate. It can take an aggressive course of psychological treatment combined with group support to effectively address more deeply entrenched patterns of behavior. Even if it does not rise to this level, masturbating with online porn is an isolating behavior, often done secretly, that involves directing one's sexual energy, desire and arousal toward people other than one's partner. And as in Rick's case, it can influence one's sexual expectations, preferences, style and presence. If you are watching one scene after another of anal sex or ejaculations on faces or threesomes or high-risk sexual scenarios, or hairless genitals, then these things can start to seem normal even if they have never been part of your sexual enjoyment. Granted, for some people, this exposure may be a springboard into a new area of sexual enjoyment[12]. But for many others, it skews their perceptions of normalcy and unrealistically raises the sexual expectations they have of their partner.

If you are wondering if it might be fun to watch some porn together, consider this: It might be. But if one of you does not find this idea appealing, that should be enough to nix it (and without judging that person's reluctance negatively). However, if both of you *really* want to do this together, be aware of the potential to become dependent on porn to make your sex life feel exciting. Even if it does provide a short-term boost, you may need increasing levels of envelope-pushing sexual behavior on screen to get the same boost going forward. Take a moment to discuss this topic openly before moving into the next chapter[13].

---

[12] In all our years of successfully helping couples enhance their sex lives, we have never found it necessary of advisable to recommend porn.

[13] For a highly informative website on porn's effects, visit www.yourbrainonporn.com.

For a complete listing of internet filtering/accountability products, visit www.sexualrecovery.com

Chapter Four

CoupleFlow Step Four:
Create Your Vision

Have you ever been driving along (in a pre-GPS world) so lost that your mind was seemingly incapable of thinking of anything other than how lost you were? You were probably mired in frustration, maybe even some fear. You were not thinking clearly about your destination because you were so consumed by

> *What distinguishes mutually satisfying relationships is each partner's ability to sustain focus on a shared, positive vision in the midst of life's obstacles.*

the fact that you were lost. You were not thinking consciously, but merely reacting *un*consciously, allowing your fear and frustration to lead you further and further into the problem. Your options shrank, you focused on whose fault it was that you were lost, and your mind swam in a churning sea of negativity.

It's easy to get lost in relationships. By its very nature, life can always be counted on to present a steady stream of challenging twists, turns, blind spots and seemingly dead-ends. All of that

> *The mere thought of this vision can generate strong feelings of trust, hope, confidence and passion.*

comes with the territory when you agree to be part of a long-term, committed relationship. What distinguishes mutually satisfying relationships is each partner's ability to sustain focus on a *shared, positive vision*[14] even while in the midst of life's steady stream of obstacles. With this focus you are able to consistently remind yourself that you are united in this world by your commitment to each other, your

---

[14] Harville Hendrix's *"Getting the Love You Want,"* persuasively articulates the need for this type of shared vision.

shared values and by the steadfast belief that everything you experience together -- from painful challenges to mountaintop highs -- can somehow be incorporated into the shared legacy you are in the process of creating.

You know what this legacy is because you have taken the time to slow down and think about what you want to create together. You can see yourself thriving in your relationship. You feel fortunate that your partner really knows you (warts and all) and accepts you for who you are. This knowing acceptance is mutual, and you know that together you can handle anything that comes your way. You see your selves truly enjoying each other, laughing together, and exchanging acts of kindness. Your connection also flows through your Bedroom, where your sexual intimacy is fun, relaxed and *very* satisfying. You respect each other's individuality while appreciating all that you share together.

The mere thought of this vision can generate strong feelings of hope, trust, passion and confidence. It is a stabilizing force even in times of unpredictability or challenging conditions. It is like *GPS for relationships*, always pointing the way home, no matter how far off course you realize you have gone. The following PIE is the first of several exercises designed to help you clarify your vision for your thriving coupleship.

Hello & Goodbye

Why This Matters:

At any time in your relationship, you have the option of reevaluating what is working for you and what is not. You get to decide what you wish to bid farewell to and what you would like to welcome into your relationship. When you do, you empower yourself to deliberately affect positive change for yourself and for your relationship. By carefully considering your relationship dynamics as well as your individual tendencies or preferences, you can re-write your relationship story as you go along. As you do, keep in mind that perfect agreement is not the goal: Sharing your perceptions with your partner is an act of intimacy, even if you don't see things exactly the same way.

Guidelines: Each of you will make three brief lists:

- On the "Goodbye" list, think of anything that has not been working for you in the relationship. These can be specific relationship dynamics ("late night arguing"), or personal tendencies of yours ("losing my temper") or your partner's ("eye rolling during conflicts"). So this list comprises all the things you would really like to see disappear from your relationship.
- On the "Hello" list, think about things from the opposite perspective: What do you think you and/or your relationship would benefit from if it was added or if there was more of it? Again, think in terms of your relationship dynamics ("more fun, more laughing, more affection,

~ 147 ~

reinstate Date Night," etc.), your perspective on yourself ("to be more present when you're telling me about your day") and your perspective on your partner ("for you to let me know when you need help or are running thin emotionally so I don't have to guess"). So this list contains the things you would gladly and enthusiastically welcome into your relationship.

- Finally, make a list of anything you would like to *retain* from your current relationship ("The way we leave love notes for each other.")

Here is a sample.

HELLO	***GOOD BYE***
1. Regular date night	1. Late night arguing
2. Eye contact when you are talking with me	2. Eye rolling
	3. Negative assumptions
3. Going to bed at or near the same time	4. Morning testiness
4. More affection	

KEEP
1. Discussing current events
2. Hiking on weekends
3. Supporting each other's interests and friendships
4. Saying "Thank you" when we help each other

Share your lists with each other. Do so without judgment of each other, but with appreciation for the thought your partner has given to this exercise. Know that you have just taken an important step in intentionally giving your relationship new direction.

Past, Present and Future

> *"... And every day that you want to wake up, you can. And every day that you want to change, I'll help you see it through."*
> *– Foster the People*

Why This Matters:

The title of this PIE refers to the three dimensions of time that shape your vision for your relationship. Vision work most obviously involves looking to the future, but having a solid grasp of your relationship's history allows you to identify problematic patterns as well as areas of strength. When you do identify problems, the key is not to wallow in them, but to spend enough time addressing them as partners so you can move into solutions. Similarly, knowing your present experience of things allows you to make adjustments where necessary, to reinforce what is working well and to know where you are currently so you can find yourself on your new map.

Guidelines:

- Reflect on the following aspects of your relationship in terms of the way you have experienced them in the past, the way you experience them in the present and the way you hope to experience them in the future.
- Get together with your partner to share your responses. Remember that you are sharing to be known better by your partner. You are listening so you may know your partner better. This is not a time to criticize what your partner shares with you, but to thank your partner for letting you in.

Here is an example for "Trust."

"In the past, I trusted you implicitly with everything. Presently, I trust you in most areas, but I really struggle to trust you in certain areas, like spending money and following through on promises. But I hope to experience more trust in these departments in the future, and I think it's normal to have some areas where the trust level varies."

1. *Trust*

2. *Emotional Connection*

3. *Communication (resolving conflicts, sharing respectfully about things that matter, etc.)*

4. Negotiating Compromise

5. Fun/Joy Together

6. Romance

7. Sexual Intimacy

Seeing Eye to Eye[15]

> *"Those eyes drew me in from the moment we first met."*
> *-Franklin, 59*

Why this Matters:

The experience of gazing deeply into a lover's eyes has long been romanticized in movies and TV. In fact, scientific research has demonstrated a very strong correlation between looking directly into someone's eyes and having increased positive feelings for that person (Williams & Kleinke, 1993). The reason is that the right hemispheres of your brains, where your emotions reside and where bonding occurs, are highly activated during an experience like this. This PIE allows you to connect intimately with each other -- right hemisphere to right hemisphere -- by maintaining direct eye contact and also by synchronizing your breathing. However connecting this may be, syncing up in this way triggers feelings of vulnerability for many people. This is because your eyes are windows to your soul. As such, extended eye contact involves each of you allowing the other to *look inside* and therefore is loaded with the potential for big feelings. A good rule of thumb is to make room for all of them as you engage in interpersonal co-regulation.

Similarly, the physical act of breathing is something we typically don't give much thought to, yet it holds enormous potential to regulate our minds and bodies. When it is *experienced consciously with your partner*, it can open up new dimensions of resonance and intimacy. Eye contact and conscious breathing are two proven

---

[15] For more on eye contact's intimately connecting power we recommend David Schnarch's *"Passionate Marriage."*

methods for enhancing intimacy and can be consistently integrated into the rest of the PIEs in this chapter.

Guidelines[16]:

- Choose a room in your home that is peaceful and private.
- Just before beginning the experience, set a timer for a period of time to which you both agree (3-5 minutes can be enough for your first time).
- Begin by facing each other, either sitting or lying down, and then start the timer.
- Breathe deeply as you look into your partner's eyes.
- Focus on your breathing to center yourself so you are as presently aware of your experience as possible. Try to synchronize your breathing with your partner as you notice whatever it is that you are feeling.
- More than anything, allow yourself to *see* your partner. Of course you see him/her right there in front of you, but what else do you see? Kindness? Vulnerability? Trust? Sadness? Courage? Do you see the person you originally fell in love with? Do you see the person you choose to love every day?
- If something distracts you (or if you come down with a case of the giggles), just refocus yourselves and continue on -- this does not need to be done perfectly!
- Feel free to end this experience by embracing each other with a hug.

ADVANCED OPTION: Do this PIE again, but choose a single word to concentrate on as you gaze at each other. Focusing on words like *"trust," "love" "partner" "open" "care"*

---

[16] Some people may find this PIE very challenging. If this pertains to you, consider trying this PIE with a single candle lighting the room, then move up to two candles the next time, and gradually working up to a softly lit room.

"compassion" and *"kind"* can make for an even more powerful connection.

Talk about it:

- What was the best part of this experience?
- What was your sense of your partner during this experience?
- What feelings and thoughts were you aware of?
- Did you experience any obstacles or distractions?
- Did anything surprise you about this experience?

Rate it:_____

Sensual Bathing

Why This Matters:

Taking a bath or shower together is something you may already be familiar with. However, this PIE is designed to be qualitatively different from your previous experiences for a very simple reason…when you slow things down, your experience of the activity changes. This is designed to be primarily a *sensual* experience and not just for washing up. As you slow down and caress each other's bodies in a sensual (and soapy) way, you may notice a new appreciation of some aspects of your partner's body as well as appreciation for being washed in such a caring way. The goal here is simply to welcome whatever positive feelings are there. We suggest beginning all the sensual PIEs with a bath or shower, so you will soon have a lot of practice!

Guidelines:

- You will take turns washing and caressing each other (in your tub or shower, wherever you are most comfortable) being mindful of the "Bikini Rule" at this stage. This means that anything that would be covered by a bikini is not yet included in the washing or caressing. By keeping the focus off of sexual parts, the Bikini Rule facilitates a more *sensual* experience.
- As the caresser, you can wash and caress your partner's hair and body. Allow yourself to get lost in your enjoyment of your partner's body. You can assume that

your partner is enjoying the washing and caressing unless you hear otherwise.

- As the receiver, let your partner know whenever you would like him/her to do something differently. Let each other know when you are ready to switch roles and also when you are ready to get out and dry each other.

Talk about it:

- What did you enjoy the most?
- Would you choose to do this again, and if so, would you make any modifications?
- What feelings *were* you aware of? What are your feelings toward your partner now?

*Rate it:*_____

Body Caress

> *"I've always loved my wife's body, but I don't usually get to savor it like this."*
> *-Mitch, 57*

Why This Matters:

You are continuing to increase your capacity to slow things down to cultivate greater presence and appreciate a broad range of sensual pleasure. You are also continuing to trust that sharing your preferences with each other adds to your enjoyment and is itself a welcomed act of intimacy. It might be that you are less familiar with some of the deliciously satisfying appetizers available on the menu of pleasurable touch than you are with the main entrées. In PIEs such as this one, you are clearly adding to the menu of pleasurable items available to you in your Bedroom. In fact, you might find that the appetizers you sometimes (or often) skip over make the entrees even *more* satisfying.

Guidelines:

- You will be caressing each other over your entire bodies, using the type of sensual touch you have been experimenting with during the previous PIEs.
- The "Bikini Rule" is in effect, meaning that any area that would be covered by bikini is off-limits for this PIE. This approach promotes exploring the potential for sensual pleasure and emotional connection that various areas of your bodies may possess beyond your breasts and genitals.
- We suggest beginning with a relaxing bath or shower together, just as you did in the Sensual Bathing PIE. Because this activity is a prelude to this PIE, it is fine to

have a shorter period of bathing/showering than in the Sensual Bathing PIE.

- Choose a place where you can be comfortable lying down (bed, couch, blanket on floor).
- As the receiver, find a position that feels comfortable while lying face down, then communicate to the caresser that you are ready. Be mindful of your touch preferences while being caressed and verbalize them to your partner. Let your partner know when you are ready to have the front of your body caressed, then turn over.
- As the caresser, enjoy caressing your partner's body, from head to toe. Remember to assume that your partner is enjoying your touch unless s/he redirects you.
- Let each other know when you are ready to switch roles (receiver becomes caresser, caresser becomes receiver).
- It may be challenging to abide by the Bikini Rule. If so, please understand that the purpose of the Bikini Rule is to promote staying connected with what you *have* in the present moment, which hopefully is an enhanced sense of your own touch preferences and a strong connection with each other through touch.

Talk about it:

- What did you enjoy the most?
- Would you like to incorporate any aspects of this PIE into your lovemaking?
- Did you encounter any barriers? If so, would you suggest any changes?
- What feelings *were* you aware of? What are your feelings toward your partner now?

*Rate it:*_____

Our Legacy

> *"What are we really going for together?*
> *I'm glad we stepped off the treadmill*
> *for a minute to think about it."*
> *-Anthony, 37*

Why This Matters:

The hectic demands of everyday life make it difficult to slow down enough to consider how and why you are choosing to live as you are and what the lasting effects of those approaches may be. You serve yourself and your relationship well when you take the time to examine your personal integrity and goals. Looking for gaps between your ideals and how you are presently living allows you to take steps to close the gaps and bring yourself back into alignment. You are creating a legacy in your relationship with each moment in each day, whether you are aware of it or not. The extent to which you *are* aware has a strong influence on creating a legacy of which you can be proud.

Guidelines:

Consider the following questions and statements:

1. **What kind of atmosphere in your relationship are you actively trying to create?**
   ("I am actively working on creating an atmosphere of loving partnership, optimism, romance, fun and trust.")

2. **Specifically, how are you going about it?**

3. **What really matters to me in this relationship is…**

4. **If there is one issue of mine that I need to work on so it does not sabotage my intended legacy it would be…**

5. **Specifically, this is what I'm doing to guard against it:**

6. **I want to be the kind of person you…**

*****

Reflect on your responses to the above questions and use them to guide you in responding to perhaps the biggest question of all, the one that underscores the preciousness of your brief time in this world with your partner…

7. *When all is said and done, I would like you to be able to say this about me:*

As True as It Gets

> *"I never thought I needed to hear anything like this from him, but when I did it was pretty powerful."*
> *-Rose, 35*

Why This Matters:

Now that you have articulated a clear vision of your ideal relationship, you are in position to energize and strengthen it. The most powerfully efficient way to harness the power of your vision is to create affirmations directly from it. Everyone has heard *Saturday Night Live* guru Stuart Smalley's infamous mantra: *"I'm good enough, I'm smart enough and doggone it, people like me."* This was a huge laugh line for the show, but the grain of truth within it is that affirmations can be extremely powerful.

Affirmations are intended to capture basic truths that by their very nature will support you, ground you and lead you toward abundance. They epitomize the practice of living in the present and living from a position of gratitude. Affirmations can neutralize our typical fears and doubts. They can lower the volume of the unproductive background noise of our minds. The transformative and empowering nature of affirmations has been well-established on an individual level through thousands of years across many cultures throughout the world. Less well-known but every bit as powerful are *couples' affirmations*.

Guidelines:

*Think of at least three statements that could serve as affirmations for your coupleship. The only criteria are that they be positive and true. Write them down, and then share them with each other by saying them out loud. Here are some examples.

My partner is on my side.

We are a great team.

My partner wants the best for me and I want the best for my partner.

We can rebound from conflicts and come through them stronger than ever.

We can ask each other directly for what we want.

Focusing on my stuff instead of on my partner's stuff helps me and our relationship.

I am grateful for my partner's love, humor, friendship, support and kindness.

I deserve to enjoy this relationship, and so does my partner.

I appreciate my partner's hard work.

I am hopeful about our future.

We don't always have to have everything figured out as long as we are in this together.

We both have good intentions, even if we miss the mark from time to time.

We still get to flirt and be romantic.

*After you each share your affirmations, commit to continuing this process in the future so your relationship can benefit from this powerful tool in an ongoing way.

Chapter Five

CoupleFlow Step Five:
Prepare to Repair

The mark of a healthy relationship is NOT the absence of conflict and differences. If you are in a truly intimate relationship with someone, with each of you consistently being honest with each other, how could your realities *not* differ, at least occasionally? These differences are to be expected -- they simply come with the territory of long-term, committed relationships. What truly defines a healthy relationship is respectful communication of differences and a consistent ability to repair when misunderstandings and/or disrespectful interactions lead to hurt feelings.

You are probably well aware that differences sometimes lead to outright conflicts. This happens when you momentarily forget about healthy boundaries and respond to your differences in Children's Menu-like ways (condescension, defensiveness, sarcasm, yelling, name-calling, eye-rolling, avoiding, etc). During these low moments, a rupture in your connection occurs. While no one looks forward to such negative interactions, they actually present an *opportunity for intimacy if repair is done well.* And since it is not realistic to practice boundaries

> *What truly defines a healthy relationship is respectful communication of differences and a consistent ability to repair when feelings are hurt.*

perfectly and to always choose from the Adult Menu, you can expect plenty of opportunities in the future!

While high-intensity conflicts tend to surface easily and spontaneously, meaningful, well-done repair rarely does. Like anything else that is important, relational repair requires some advance planning. Have you ever taken some non-conflict time to actually plan how you will be better partners during and after your next disagreement? If so, you are likely to:

- spend less time and energy in anger and resentment
- feel greater levels of connection in your relationship
- risk being vulnerable the next time because you trust that your partnership can handle rough spots and difficult conversations

The rest of this chapter guides you in strengthening your plan and skills for repair while continuing to blend in some Bedroom fun. You are sure to notice a strengthening flow between your Living Room and Bedroom.

What's Your Conflict Style?

> *"We complement each other perfectly.*
> *He shuts down when I get mad and I*
> *get mad when he shuts down."*
> *-Monica, 63*

Why This Matters:

Every couple has room to improve the way they relate with each other before, during and after conflict. The first step is to identify your typical conflict styles. Knowing your own natural tendencies puts you in a better position to get beyond the ones you identify as unhelpful. Knowing your partner's tendencies can help you to take things less personally, even as you may ask your partner to do some things differently.

Guidelines:

Answer the following questions:

1. **When you and your partner are *not* practicing boundaries as adults and are not expressing your differences relationally, what does that usually look like?** ("I raise my voice, you withdrawal" "I'm ready to move on, but you want to keep talking about something, then we both escalate" "Zero to 60 in no time flat, then the silent standoff begins")

2. **If you just did what comes most *naturally* to you, how would you describe your typical conflict style?** (Do you avoid? Do you get aggressive? Do you use your superior rational arguing skills? Do you shut down at a certain point? Do you try to reason? Do you apologize quickly to end the conflict? Do you blame? Do you defend yourself?)

3. **What do you typically do in the wake of conflict?** (Apologize? Demand an apology? Initiate discussion about the conflict? Pretend it didn't happen? Avoid/withdraw?)

4. **What has worked well for you in the past when in conflict (or potential conflict) with your partner?**

5. **What has your partner done that has been helpful in past conflicts?**

Choose a time to share your responses to with each other, then move on to the next PIE.

Body Talk

*"I'm more aware than ever of just how far
back my body image feelings go."*
-Michelle, 51

Why This Matters:

No touching is involved in this PIE, just a quick way to help you identify your perceptions and feelings about your bodies and to share them with each other. This exercise can be challenging if you are one of the many people who are either disconnected from their bodies or who have negative feelings about them. If so, this PIE presents an excellent opportunity to know your partner more fully and to allow yourself to be more fully known. This is *exactly* how to cultivate intimacy. So be sure to let your partner know if you're feeling nervous or uncomfortable with this one. Even if you have a positive body image, this PIE can still be a great way to learn more about each other.

Guidelines:

Answer the following sentence completion items on your own, and then share your responses with your partner.

1. The part of my body I feel best about is my_____
   because _____.
2. The part of my body I feel worst about is my
   _____ because _____.
3. In my mind, I imagine that when you see my naked body
   you think, "_____."
4. (Men) I have always thought that my penis is
   _____.

5. (Women) I have always thought that my vagina is

   _____.

6. When you see me naked I feel_____.

7. When I was younger, I felt most secure about my

   _____.

8. When I was younger, I felt most insecure about my

   _____.

9. I had the most positive feelings about my body when I was
   ___ years old because… _____.

10. I had the most negative feelings about my body when I was
    ___ years old because… _____.

11. The part of my body that has changed the most through the
    years is my _____.

12. The part of my body I'm most concerned about as I think
    about getting older is my _____.

13. Something I could be doing differently to feel better about
    my body is _____.

14. The part of your body I like the best is your
    _____ (and a close second would be your
    _____).

*****

Notice how it felt to let each other in during this exercise. Let your partner know how you are feeling toward him/her right now.

Adult Show & Tell

Why This Matters:

In this PIE, you are going to be giving a presentation on the sexual and erotic parts of your body to your partner. Odds are you have never done anything quite like this before, so you'll have to trust us that this exercise can provide a significant boost to your Bedroom. This PIE holds tremendous value from a practical standpoint, allowing you to *teach* each other about the specifics of your sexual anatomy. This level of specificity is important because no matter how much sexual knowledge or experience one has, there is a wide range of differences among people. The good news is that you don't need to be an expert in Male/Female Sexual Preferences. What is most important is to be an expert guide regarding *your* sexual preferences and to be an open-minded student regarding your *partner's* sexual preferences. This PIE is more clinical than any of the others. It aims to support you in becoming more comfortable using specific names for sexual anatomy and provides opportunities for each of you to ask questions about the other's body and about sexual experience.

Letting each other in on your private parts in a direct and clear way usually carries with it some feelings of vulnerability and therefore has increased intimacy potential. Because this experience is designed to be specific and detailed, you might feel awkward, fearful or resistant. Therefore, you may notice that entering into this experience with your partner requires tremendous trust.

Guidelines:

- In privacy, take a moment to examine your own genitals. Women may find it helpful to use a hand mirror to assist with an easier view. Make mental notes regarding what types of touch (if any) are most pleasurable for each of these parts. Also notice any feelings that may be triggered by this experience. Please be aware that it is not uncommon to have some negative emotions surface if you were raised with sex-negative messages, or if you have been abused or have had prior negative sexual experiences.

- The interactive part of this PIE can occur in any room in which you can be comfortable and have privacy.

- The person who is *most* comfortable with this PIE should be the first presenter. (If you're equally comfortable, just flip a coin!)

- The presenting partner chooses a comfortable position, and begins identifying each specific part of his/her genitals. Assume that your partner *knows nothing* about your preferences.

- Women should specifically identify and discuss sensory experiences with the following: Outer and inner labia, vaginal and urethral openings, perineum and clitoris. Women should also use the same process with their breasts, specifically discussing sensory experiences with their nipples and aureoles.

- Men should specifically identify the following: frenulum, glans, coronal ridge and shaft of their penis. Men should use the same process with their testicles, scrotum and perineum, specifically discussing sensory experiences.

- Use clinical names in order to increase your comfort level in talking directly about these parts of your anatomies and to improve the accuracy of your sexual communication. You are more likely to know what the other is describing or asking for if you both use the same language. Of course, you always have the option of substituting "pet" names for clinical names -- just as long as you each know what the other means!

- As the presenting partner, you also have the option of discussing non-sexual areas of your body that are also pleasurable when touched. These areas can also vary widely from one person to the next. For example, it might be that spot on your neck, ear, breast, forearm, buttocks, foot, calf or ankle that you know to be an erogenous zone *for you.*

- Clarity is very important, and the best way to be clear is to supplement your verbal communication with a demonstration. It's great to say, "I prefer a light, slow, indirect touch around my clitoris," or "I like it when you play with my testicles, but not too rough," and even better to show your partner *exactly* what you mean ("Here, let me show you a great way to touch my clitoris" or ""This is my frenulum and it feels amazing to have it touched like this…"). As the listener, you can ask to touch the part being discussed in the way your partner is saying feels best.

After each of you has had a chance to present yourself to your partner, it could be a good time to thank each other for the trust that was involved in the experience you just shared together. Also discuss the thoughts and feelings you were aware of during this PIE.

Talk about it:

- What was the best aspect of this PIE?
- What was the least comfortable aspect of this PIE?
- Did you learn anything new about either your partner or yourself?

*****

If either one of you has any recent history of sexual challenges, including erectile dysfunction, premature ejaculation, arousal/orgasm difficulties and/or painful intercourse, you should be working with a Certified Sex Therapist to directly address these areas of concern. There are effective treatment protocols for these sexual problems, and the rest of the PIEs in this book will be much more enjoyable when you have made progress in these areas. Contact us via email at bill@drsbercaw.com or ginger@drsbercaw.com or use the following websites to locate a Certified Sex Therapist in your area: www.aasect.org or www.sexualwholeness.com.

Re-Writing History

Why This Matters:

One of the best ways to plan for the future is to use information from the past. This PIE will help you in transforming an argument from the past into a template for stronger partnership during conflict situations. It will also help you to clarify and refine your best practices when it comes to repairing your relationship ruptures.

Guidelines:

Think about the last conflict you had with your partner and answer the following questions:

1. How did it fall into a familiar pattern that has created ruptures in the past?

2. How would you have done things differently on *your side*?

3. What might have been helpful *from your partner's side*?

Now it's time for the re-write. Write a brief narrative about how that same scenario could have played out in a more relational manner.

Body Caress II

> *"His hands say so much about his love for me. I hope mine do the same for him."*
> -Alli, 37

Why This Matters:

If you're still not convinced that slowing things down can really spice things up, here's a PIE that's sure to increase your odds of being a believer. This PIE gives you another opportunity to enjoy each other's body, just for the sake of enjoying each other's body. The biggest difference you'll notice between this body caress and the one in the previous chapter is that the Bikini Rule has gone by the wayside. Keep in mind that while this PIE allows you to *incorporate* the sexual parts of your bodies into this caressing experience, the goal is not to *focus* on them. Remember to let your love of your partner's body be your guide while caressing.

Guidelines:

- You will be taking turns caressing and being caressed all over your bodies, including (but not focusing on) the breasts and genitals.
- Consider beginning this PIE by enjoying a sensual bath or shower together.
- The first receiver finds a position that feels comfortable while lying face down.
- As the *receiver*, be mindful of your touch preferences and verbalize them to your partner. Let your partner know when you are ready to have the front of your body caressed, then turn over.
- As the *caresser*, you can simply enjoy caressing your partner's body, from head to toe. Remember to assume that your partner is enjoying the touch unless s/he redirects you.

- After enjoying this caressing, either of you may express when you are ready to switch roles (receiver becomes caresser, caresser becomes receiver).

Talk about it:
- What did you enjoy the most?
- Did you encounter any barriers? If so, would you want to make any modifications?
- What feelings were you aware of? What are your feelings toward your partner now?

Rate it:_____

Excuses, Excuses…

At this stage of the *CoupleFlow* program, you have had many opportunities to navigate the tricky issue of planning your PIEs into the rest of your busy lives. Ideally, each of your strong commitments to showing up for your planned times is balanced with an understanding that in certain situations, plans may need to be adjusted. There are so many things that can get in the way of your well-intentioned plans. Everything from physical issues (fatigue, illness, injury) to unexpected circumstantial changes (car trouble, children's needs, last minute social invitations, client meetings running late, business deadlines that get moved up, etc.) can really throw your plans off track. When you are tired and busy, the *easiest thing to postpone is your time together.*

Sometimes you may decide to simply push your PIE start time back a little later. But other times, one or both of you may prefer to reschedule. Rescheduling is part of life, but when it becomes the norm it can send an unintentional message that you are not giving your best effort. Thoughtfully talking about any time challenges you are facing goes a long way toward promoting a spirit of partnership. It reinforces that you are still very much invested in showing up and growing closer, despite your need to promoting a spirit of partnership. It reinforces that you are still very much invested in showing up and growing closer, despite your need to change plans. Sometimes a pattern emerges related to postponing PIEs. For example, you may seem more likely to postpone when your start time is after 9PM, or on Wednesdays, or on the same day as a weekly staff meeting. So take a moment to consider the following questions:

- How would you rate your follow-through on keeping your scheduled PIE times?
- How is your approach to planning time together similar/different from your partner's?

- What are some of the most common scheduling challenges you face personally?
- What are some of the most common scheduling challenges that your partner faces?
- Do you notice any patterns regarding postponement of your PIE times?
- Are there any adjustments you would like to suggest that might improve your scheduling success rate?

Love Means...Knowing How to Say "I'm Sorry"

> *"It can be so hard for him to apologize, but it's so helpful when he does."*
> -Stacey, 52

Why This Matters:

Do you know what it's like to be locked in an emotional stare-down with your partner, each of you firmly committed to how right you are and how wronged you've been? In that moment, it might go against your grain, but a solid option always available to you is simply to own your part in the conflict and to offer a genuine apology. Another is to ask for an apology when you believe that would be helpful to you. So what makes for a good apology? A good apology has three main components.

1. *Acknowledging the offensive behavior* ("I know I was insensitive to approach you with those words I used.")
2. *Expressing empathy for your partner* ("I can understand why you were so upset -- it must not have been very pleasant to be on the receiving end.")
3. *Committing to refrain from offensive behavior* ("I've got to do a better job of protecting you from that kind of thing." "I'm going to be much more aware of this going forward.")

A good apology NEVER involves the following:

1. *Quid Pro Quo* (e.g., "I'll apologize <u>if</u> you agree never to 'X' again.")
2. *Justifying the offensive behavior* ("I'm sorry for 'X', but when you did 'Y' it just made me see red.")
3. *Asking anything of your partner* ("So will you forgive me?" "Can you stop crying now?" "So aren't *you* going to apologize for anything?")

4. *Placing responsibility for being offended onto your partner* ("I'm sorry if you took it the wrong way.")

This PIE is designed to help you plan for the next time you either need to apologize for some offensive behavior or need to ask for an apology from your partner -- or both.

Guidelines:

1. **So many of your expectations, attitudes and behaviors around apology can be traced back to what was modeled for you in your childhood environment. With that in mind, consider the following questions**.
   - How was apology handled in the family you were raised in?
   - Did the adults ever apologize to each other or to the children?
   - Were children asked to apologize to the adults and each other?
   - How did apologies in your family compare with the apology do's and don'ts in the previous page?
   - What factors in your childhood do you think have shaped your feelings about apology?

2. **Think about what characterizes a meaningful apology to you** (use the guidelines on the previous page if they are helpful to you). If you could script it out, what would it sound like? Write that script in the space below and then share your script with your partner.

ON THE LOOKOUT

Though many conflicts seem to happen spontaneously, every couple has their own, well-established hot spots. These are the situations that have led to ruptures in the past, and are likely to do so again if there is no advance planning to be better partners to each other. It could be chronic conflict around getting the kids ready for school or getting them to bed. Major events like birthdays and holidays as well as visits from family are classic conflict triggers. Sometimes it all comes together in a big package of emotional quicksand and all of a sudden, there you are, ordering from the Children's Menu.

Take the case of Manny and Calista. Despite the fact that their modest home really could not comfortably accommodate guests, Manny's parents never failed to invite themselves to spend a week with them every Christmas. Calista deferred to Manny year after year because she knew how much it meant to him to see his parents at this time of year. But if history repeated itself, it would only be a day or two into their visit before the tension between Manny and Calista would be palpable. Calista felt like her house was not her own at the very time of year that she most wanted it to feel like it was.

Perhaps it was sleeping on an air mattress so her in-laws could be more comfortable in their room. Perhaps it was the inconvenience of sharing a bathroom and kitchen with them. Perhaps it was a week's worth of syncing schedules with them. All she knew was that this was not the way she envisioned spending her precious holiday time with her husband and two young children. Sometimes she would try to steal a private moment to vent to Manny. Manny would typically react defensively ("What am I supposed to do, just kick them out?") and Calista would feel hurt and storm off.

Instead of just bracing for the inevitable while hoping somehow this year would be different, Calista decided to try a different approach, based on the *CoupleFlow* model of communicating. In early September, before any plans had been discussed with his parents, she approached Manny:

Calista: "Do you have a few minutes to talk? It's something that's important to me."

Manny: "Of course I can talk, what's going on?"

Calista: "This is a difficult one for me...I can feel my heart beating pretty fast right now, so I know I'm a little nervous, but here goes: Is it OK if we talk about the holidays?"

Manny: "Well, thanks for telling me what it is. I was afraid something was really wrong!"

Calista: "No, no, I'm sorry to scare you. It's just that I've had a lot of fear about this conversation. When I think about the holidays, I feel a lot of anxiety and uncertainty instead of the excitement I'd like to feel. I'd really like to partner with you to find a way for us both to enjoy the holidays -- would you be open to that?"

Manny: "Look, I think I get what you're saying -- I know having my parents with us changes some things. But it's still really important to me to see them during that week."

Calista: "Absolutely -- and I get that. I'd like to find a way so that can still happen. But I need to be honest with you about my reality. I am not interested in spending another Christmas Eve on the air mattress and sharing a bathroom. I hope you can understand, it's the whole process of having anyone in our house for that length of time and at that time of year...it's really exhausting and it takes me away from so many of the moments I'd like to enjoy with you and the kids."

Manny: "OK, I hear you. I know what you're talking about and I agree, it hasn't been easy. But I'm not sure exactly what you are asking."

Calista: "Again, I'm a little nervous to put this out there, but I'd like us to tell them what would work better for us. From my perspective, it would be OK if they stayed with us for a few days after Christmas. I'd be fine with them arriving in town a couple days before Christmas like usual, but I'd like to have our house to ourselves during that time. That would mean they'd be staying in a hotel. What do you think?"

Manny: "I think their feelings would be hurt. I'm afraid they might not even come at all if we tell them they're not welcome here."

Calista: "Well, I hope that wouldn't be their response, and just to clarify, that certainly wouldn't be my message, that they're not welcome. I'd like to communicate that we would love to see them over the holidays, but that we need to make an adjustment in how we set up that time."

Manny: "Uh huh."

Calista: "Manny, I see you looking far away right now and I'm thinking that you are really uncomfortable with what I'm suggesting. I'm a little concerned."

Manny: "It's true, I am uncomfortable. But I think I knew this day was coming. It's not like it's easy on me either, Calista. But I can imagine it's been even harder on you. I just have a lot of fear about how they would react. I think that's why I'm looking away. But looking at you, I can see who I should be most focused on.."

Calista: "Manny, I had no idea -- thanks for letting me know all that."

Manny: "Yeah, sure. But I'd like to talk about how this would look- what we'd be proposing and how it might work, practically speaking. I mean, I need to know more about what you'd still be comfortable with. Like would you be OK with them being here for meals and the kids' bedtimes if they were at a hotel?"

Calista: "Yes, I would, as long as they have their own place to stay. I think I might actually enjoy being around them more!"

Manny: "Yeah, to be honest, maybe I would too."

Calista: "Manny, this conversation is so hopeful. We're talking about something that's been pretty loaded for both of us and I think we're really doing well. This is exactly the kind of partnership I'd like to have during that week. Where *we* come first and we're really there for each other. I'm willing to do whatever I can to meet you there."

Manny: "That sounds really good to me too. Just try to understand, this is not going to be easy for me, telling my parents they need to get a room."

Calista: "I know. And I'd like to be there for the conversation, too, if you think that would be alright. That way you won't have to do this by yourself."

Manny and Calista are on their way to preparing for a holiday season like no other. Look at how they got there: Calista could no longer ignore this hot spot, and she thought about how to bring it to Manny in a way that was *true to herself and respectful of him.* Manny stayed tuned in to her, even in the face of what had to be a challenging request to hear. They slowed themselves down, stayed on the Adult's Menu, and walked away with another layer of trust and intimacy.

A Hands-On Lesson

"I loved the feeling of his hand under mine, making all the right moves in all the right places. It was great to see how interested he was in what I liked."
-Claire, 39

Why This Matters:

This PIE is a great complement to the *"Adult Show and Tell"* you completed earlier. It will help you take another step toward directly teaching your partner about your touch preferences as well as learning about your partner's preferences. Just as you recently were able to give and receive a "lesson" on the erotic and sexual areas of your bodies, in this PIE you will expand this to include your entire bodies.

Part of your progress so far involves enhancing self-awareness of your sensual/sexual preferences and conditions. As your self-awareness grows, you are taking ownership of *your* responsibility for *your* own pleasure. The basic premise is: *If you really want your partner to know what you like, you're going to need to show him/her!* Accepting this premise, you continue to communicate your preferences clearly. Allowing yourselves the vulnerability associated with this level of communication rewards you with a more intimate understanding of each other's experiences. You are again being very proactive about deepening the intimacy and trust in your relationship. The goal for each of you is to be as comfortable as possible while serving as your partner's personal guide to your sensual and sexual preferences. Though the teaching/learning component of this PIE may be similar to the *"Adult Show and Tell,"* this PIE is less clinical. It is also an opportunity for each of you to ask questions about your partner's physical and sexual experience.

Guidelines:

- Enjoy a bath or shower together as a relaxing warm-up for this PIE.

- As the person giving the first lesson, find a comfortable position, invite your partner to join you, then guide your partner's hands all over and around your body.

- You may wish to have your partner's hand resting on top of yours or to have his/her hand under yours (skin to skin).

- Demonstrate as clearly as possible the type of touch that feels best to you. So if you prefer a light, circular touch on your shoulders or a more firm up and down touch on the sole of your foot, now is the time to show your partner exactly how you like it.

- It may be necessary to shift positions to allow access to most of your body. For your backs, you can demonstrate on each other what your preferences are.

- As the one being guided, your goal is simply to be open to the lesson. This means that you will need to relax your hands and arms so your partner can easily guide you all around his/her body. Be sure to ask questions as they come up. After the first lesson has been completed, it is time to switch roles.

- This hands-on lesson is intended to provide equal attention to all areas of the body. But since it *does* include the breasts and genitals, there certainly is the potential for arousal. Whether arousal occurs or not is irrelevant: The focus remains on the process of sharing, teaching and learning that is fundamental to *CoupleFlow* and Sexual Abundance. But if you do get aroused, certainly enjoy it!

- Keep in mind that even as you are trying to be clear in your lessons, there is likely to be some variability from one experience to the next: The same touch that feels wonderful on Sunday is not certain to have the exact same effect if repeated on Wednesday. In fact, it is that *variability that contributes to the process of renewal and experimentation that can keep your sex lives interesting.* You are not doing these lessons so you may become "perfect students." The goal is simply to develop a better understanding of some of your partner's typical preferences while leaving plenty of room to be redirected during future experiences.

- After each of you has given your hands-on lesson, there is another opportunity to express gratitude to each other for the openness and trust involved in the time you just shared.

Talk about it:

- What was the best aspect of this PIE?
- Are you aware of anything that might have helped your experience be better?
- Do you have a better sense of how you and your partner prefer to enjoy touch?
- Can you tell a difference between your comfort levels in discussing your preferences now versus when you first began this program?

Rate it:_____

GOING ON THE OFENSIVE

So far in this chapter, we've focused on preparing for difficult conversations and planning for new ways to communicate respectfully in order to deepen your intimacy. Just as important for preparing for the rough spots that you know are bound to happen, is also preparing yourselves to be in love with each other every day. Prepare to be in love? That doesn't sound very romantic.

What we mean is to do something that places your partner in two places at the same time: *the front of your mind and the center of your heart*. Many times, this means going against the flow of the day and even against the flow of your mood. In a sense, you are going on the offensive, taking charge of your mind, especially your thoughts and feelings about your partner. The next two PIEs are designed to help you start your day with each other in mind and to carry a spirit of love and grace for each other throughout the day.

> *Do something that places your partner in two places at the same time: the front of your mind and the center of your heart.*

Powering Up

Why This Matters:

The morning hours can be especially daunting in any household. Even on so-called normal mornings, it's usually a harried rush to get yourselves and your children dressed, fed, brushed, and out the door. When something unexpected is added to the mix, ("I don't know where my homework is!" "Mom!!! Aidan just threw up!") the pressure can be ratcheted up to high-risk levels. The risk is of losing sight of your partnership and reacting to each other in critical, controlling, manipulative or withdrawing ways. Even for those without children, each of you is naturally focused on all the tasks ahead of you in your day, some of which you may not be feeling all that great about. You are moments away from facing the world, and you can either do it on your own, or with a teammate.

Fortunately, you know exactly where to find your very best teammate, the one who knows you better than anyone else and the one whom you also want to support. She may be in the bathroom applying make-up or perhaps groggy in bed, just waking up. He may be getting the kids lunches together or finishing up his workout. If you are able to exchange even a brief, supportive commitment with this person, you can reinforce your places on this team, and gain strength from it. You may not know exactly what the game of life is going to challenge you with today, but you will know that you have a trusted ally in your corner.

So no matter how well you succeed in improving your relationship, every day you need to wake up and give it your best effort again. There is such a tremendous opportunity embedded in that challenge: to continue operating from an increasing position of relational strength. It's not dependent on the weather or the stock market or your boss's mood or your children's homework. It's up to you and you alone. And in return for a relatively small amount of effort (less than a minute), you and your partner receive a powerful shot in the arm that can connect you throughout your day.

Guidelines:

Do the following each morning for two weeks, then commit to making it permanent:

1. **Set your intentions regarding your partner:** This is done internally. Briefly remind yourself of your love and appreciation for your partner and what kind of influence you would like to be in his/her day.

2. **Find your partner:** Do this before your house starts to get active. Make adjustments depending on your situation. For example, if you have very young children, you may need to take these steps with one or more of them around. Or, if one of you leaves the home before the other wakes, or is away traveling, you can do this by phone.

3. **State your commitment to your partner:** Be very clear in your communication that you are carrying your partner with you today and keeping him/her in your thoughts. "I want you to know that I am with you today no matter what." "My goal is to be a great partner with you today." "I have so much love and appreciation for you, and I will be thinking of you all day." At the very least a simple "I love you" while making eye contact should always be shared before heading out the door.

Loving Gracefully

Why This Matters:

Grace allows you to accept yourself and your partner as human beings, who, despite their best intentions, are fallible and imperfect. When you stumble due to errors in judgment, carelessness or forgetfulness, or when you lack information or encounter unforeseen circumstances, you come face to face with your own very human limitations. Of course, you also quite naturally come face to face with those of your partner.

Life is challenging enough without piling on yourself or your partner. Instead of coming down on yourself and getting into unhealthy shame, ("I'm a bad person/spouse" "Of course I messed this up" "I'm such an idiot!") or coming down on your partner and getting into blame ("How could s/he be so stupid?" "We wouldn't be in this mess if only s/he would have…") it is *always your option to extend grace instead.*

Grace is not to be confused with excusing bad behavior or with denying your reality. Grace is an authentic feeling that allows you to be good to yourself and others, especially under difficult circumstances. It also allows you to get off of your partner's side of the street where you are more likely to criticize and nitpick. It allows you to look beyond undesirable outcomes and to see the imperfect human being who could use a warm arm around her shoulders instead of a cold look of scorn. The path to intimacy, including joy, love and passion is paved with grace, but can be blocked by blame and resentment. The following PIE will

~ 190 ~

reinforce your power to choose. See if you feel a little lighter after responding to these questions.

Guidelines:

Answer the following questions, then share your responses with your partner.

1. **Think about a recent time when you came down too hard on yourself. What was the negative thought running through your mind? How would it have looked if you were treating yourself with grace instead of shame?** ("I overdrew our checking account again because I forgot to move money over from our other account. I told myself I'm an idiot, I'm not responsible, I can't even handle the simplest tasks in life. I felt like a loser and didn't want to tell you about it. If I had been more graceful with myself I could have slowed down, taken appropriate responsibility for my error, figured out some adjustment to reduce the chance of it happening again, and told myself that I am a good person with good intentions who makes occasional mistakes.")

2. **Now follow the same format as above, but this time use an example when you came down too hard on your partner.** ("When I picked up Samantha from school she was hot and exhausted. I saw she was overdressed in long sleeves and black pants on a warm, sunny day. I was so mad at you, telling myself that you just don't get it, and that I'm on my own when it comes to looking out for this kind of thing. If I had been more graceful with you, I could have slowed down, noticed my frustration and reminded myself that you would never intend for our daughter to be anything other than comfortable, and that you probably just didn't realize how warm she would be. I'd also remind myself that I've done the same thing before!")

Bedroom Soccer
(with Post-Game Entertainment!)

Why This Matters:

You don't have to be a fan of soccer, or even sports for that matter, in order to be a big fan of this PIE. *Bedroom Soccer* is intended to be pure fun, even silly, with a lot more pleasure than you can find on the real playing field. This PIE continues to keep things light in the Bedroom as you experiment with fresh ways of enjoying each other. It is designed so you can flow right from Bedroom Soccer into the "Post-Game Entertainment." Sometimes the topic of oral sex comes up during the "No Hands" part. If so, it may present an opportunity to discuss how you each feel about oral sex, especially if this has been a tricky issue in your Bedroom. Remember to allow plenty of room for different feelings and preferences. There is no "right or wrong" way to feel about this. The important thing is to be as clear as you can in expressing your preferences and comfort level as you remain open to hearing your partner's as well.

Guidelines:

- Before beginning this PIE, again enjoy a bath or shower together. The person being caressed first lies naked with his/her back exposed.
- As the caresser, you can use any part of your body to caress your partner's body EXCEPT your hands, just like soccer - no hands allowed! Feel free to experiment by using parts of your body you would not normally use: your hair, cheeks, lips, arms, feet, chest, nose, tongue and even your

breasts and/or genitals. Be as creative as you like, as long as your partner is comfortable with what you are doing.

- As the receiver, soak it all in, then turn over to enjoy pleasuring on the front of your body in the same way.
- After each of you has had a chance in each role, it is time to move into the second part of this PIE: Soccer is over, but the *post-game entertainment* is set to begin!
- Lying closely together and facing each other, breathe deeply and look into each other's eyes for as long as you like (remember *Seeing Eye to Eye*?)
- Because it's time for some post-game entertainment, you can use your hands however you like (and don't forget about kissing!) Remember to ask for the type of touch you prefer and/or show your partner how it's done.
- Continue kissing and caressing until one or both of you would like to conclude your experience. Given the erotic and pleasurable touching involved, you may choose to follow your arousal wherever it leads you.[17]

Talk about it:

- What did you enjoy the most? How did you like the no-hands rule?
- How did the post-game simultaneous pleasuring feel different from the individual caressing you had been practicing up until now in this program?
- What feelings were you aware of? How are you feeling toward your partner now?

Rate it:_____

---

[17] If you consistently have difficulty reaching orgasm, you should consult with a Certified Sex Therapist for help with this highly treatable situation. Again, let us know if you would like to consult with us via videoconferencing if you reside outside the Los Angeles area.

Chapter Six

CoupleFlow Step Six:
Lock It In!

Now that you are nearing the end of this book, you are in a highly desirable position: Advances in the Living Room and Bedroom have created a self-reinforcing, positively charged intimacy feedback loop. Together, you have been bringing the concept of *Sexual Abundance* that you read about in Part One to life. When you look back on what you've done and you consider the rosy outlook for sustaining and even expanding your intimacy enhancements, there is much to be hopeful and grateful for.

If there is one feeling that promotes abundance as much as any other it is *gratitude*. There are many pathways to gratitude. Sometimes the simple act of reflecting on *what you have* leads to gratitude. Other times you might suddenly be struck by the awareness of some goodness in your life. Whatever the path, when you are in gratitude, you are *welcoming joy into your life*. The *CoupleFlow* model also emphasizes *fun* as a core path to experiencing joy with your partner. The winning formula that captures the link between fun, joy and gratitude is this:

- Have a *FUN, meaningful experience* together +
- Feel *JOY* in response to the experience =
- *GRATITUDE* (conscious awareness of the experience and the joy)

One simple law of nature is that *joy and gratitude must be consciously pursued, noticed, and savored,* unlike negative emotions which surface and linger much more easily. There is a Darwinian explanation for this universal human experience: Our negative emotions serve to protect us from threats, whether perceived or real. They often arise from the part of the brain that has been around since man's earliest days. It is known in layman's terms as the "reptilian brain" and its purpose today is the same as its purpose was thousands of years ago: to keep us out of harm's way. Because it is wired in this way, it operates from an *overprotection bias*, often registering a perceived sense of danger even when there is no actual basis for it. When activated, this part of the brain leads us straight to the Children's Menu, where each of the options is fear-based. The bottom line is that from an evolutionary perspective, our brains are not as concerned with *connecting us with* others as they are with *protecting us from* others. The brain is not as naturally wired to keep memories of positive experiences close to the surface as it is wired to keep painful memories easily accessible.

Think about it this way: *How many times have you been woken up by joy in the middle of the night?* The much greater likelihood is that some anxiety, sadness or guilt is likely to be an uninvited nighttime visitor. Our minds can work overtime to keep negative feelings active in our minds, even when all we want to do is sleep.

> *How many times have you been woken up by joy in the middle of the night?*

This also explains why it is easier to hang onto a grudge than to forgive, and easier to avoid difficult conversations than to enter into them directly. Our brains naturally store memories of previous hurts and disappointments, ready to be recalled the next time we encounter the person or situation associated with the hurt or disappointment.

Because our brains work in predictable ways to protect us, ways that do not necessarily promote trust and intimacy, it becomes even more important to *intentionally* make room for the good stuff like joy and gratitude. The PIEs in this next and final step have the common thread of presenting ready-made opportunities to experience gratitude. You will also be developing your own plan *(Lifetime Blueprint)* to allow you to continue to intentionally nurture your relationship in all the ways you know better now than ever that work best for you. As you continue to enjoy your expanded menu of sensually and sexually pleasurable choices, remember that it is *gratitude that provides the renewable energy between the Living Room and the Bedroom that keeps things flowing in the direction you both want.*

Make Fun #1!

> *"If there's one thing we've always done well together, it's __fun__."*
> *-Kathleen, 59*

Why This Matters:

Do you remember when you and your partner first met and began to really like each other? Were you having fun then? Of course you were. When you think about it, *your relationship was built on fun*. It's likely that your "fun time for us" has diminished in frequency since those early days. If so, there is no need for alarm, as this can be partially attributed to your relationship maturing and entering into a different stage of love.

Though the goal is not to completely recapture the *intensity* of those wonderful days gone by, the goal *is* to use the same formula for maximizing fun that helped the two of you to develop your original bond. By giving your shared fun a higher level of priority and committing to have more fun together, you can infuse novelty and joy into your relationship, no matter how long you have been together. You deserve to always be looking forward to something together -- whether a walk around the neighborhood or a trip around the world, the point is that it's the two of you sharing something you enjoy. This PIE will help you to target new (and old) ways to amplify your fun quotient together.

Guidelines Part I:

- Set a timer for *3 minutes*. During this time, each of you will make a list of ALL the activities you currently enjoy or have enjoyed doing with your partner. Think broadly and go as far back as you like.
- Place a check mark next to the fun activities that are occurring at a frequency is working just fine for you.
- Circle the activities you would like to engage more frequently. Make a separate list for activities you have not yet experienced together but that you would like to try.

Guidelines Part II:

Look at the next 30 calendar days, then discuss these questions:

- Do you see any of the Part I activities on your calendars?
- Are there any activities that are not scheduled into your calendar but that you can still count on happening? ("Our Friday night walk" "Saturday morning coffee on the patio").
- Which items would you like to add to your calendar?
- If you see activities on your lists that were fun at one time but have fallen by the wayside, would you like to suggest re-engaging them?
- If you look beyond the next 30 days, are there enough scheduled fun opportunities on the horizon? Again, would you like to add some?
- Consider how your styles of approaching fun activities differ. Does it seem that one of you tends to take the lead on suggesting or planning fun activities? Remember, different styles can be *entirely complementary*. For example, if one person is more spontaneous while the other is a planner, this can work out great if each of you is flexible enough to go back and forth between approaches.

Fun with Fantasy

"My long-standing embarrassment about my fantasy turned to exhilaration once I finally let my husband in on my idea."
-Amber, 32

Why This Matters:

We spend so much of our lives presenting ourselves in certain ways in order to be appropriate for situations and to play our various social roles. Sexual fantasy can be a wonderful way to leave these restrictions behind and really get in touch with your sexual self. It allows you to check your inhibitions at the door, as your mind envisions a highly pleasurable, erotic and arousing scenario without concern of being judged by anyone else.

There are so many possibilities for fantasy content. In this PIE, the only guideline is that any sexual content involves *only you and your partner*. The reason for this is that *CoupleFlow* is based on intimacy. We believe that anytime you direct your sexual energy, thoughts and feelings toward anyone (or anything) other than your partner, the intimacy between you and your partner gets diluted.

The goal of fantasy is to let your mind freely enjoy a creation of its own. However, this PIE also asks that you share at least one of your sexual fantasies with each other. This involves some degree of vulnerability (thus raising the intimacy potential), so be sure to respect any such feelings if they arise. Keep in mind that whenever sharing fantasies, there should be no expectation that your partner will be willing to jump right into it with you. Just as there should be no negative judgment of either of your fantasies, there should be no negative judgment of either partner's reservations about making a fantasy a reality (and sometimes the fantasy's creator is just fine with it *remaining* a fantasy to be enjoyed in his/her own mind).

Guidelines Part I:

- Write a narrative that captures at least one of your sexual fantasies involving you and your partner.
- Be as descriptive as possible (even if it starts sounding like a bad romance novel!). Describe the *setting* including all of the sights, sounds and smells. Also describe the *context* of the scenario as this is often a major component of the fantasy (some element of surprise or something that runs counter to societal role expectations). Have fun with this!

Guidelines Part II:

- Read your fantasies aloud to each other. Be sure to let each other know if you are nervous or embarrassed to share.
- When you've each had a chance to share, discuss how you might like to explore this fantasy, if at all. For example, one husband was surprised (pleasantly) to learn that his wife fantasized about them making love in their backyard. They decided to try it the following weekend and were so glad they did! Another woman's fantasy involved seducing her partner in the lobby of the hotel she was staying at for business, having her way with him back in her room, then seeing him in the audience of the class she was teaching the next day. She knew it wasn't realistic to role play this one *exactly*, but it got them talking about some fun variations of it!
- These examples illustrate the intended spirit of this PIE: Let your mind go wherever it likes while withholding judgment and expectations. This will maximize your fun with fantasy!
  Rate it:_____

STAYING CONNECTED IN THE BEDROOM

Do you recall earlier in this book when we discussed the concept of slowing things down to spice things up? Since you've made it this far, you have a lot of experience with this philosophy! Hopefully, you also have an expanded menu of pleasurable activities to continue integrating into your Bedroom time. You are also likely to have enhanced feelings of presence when you are together. Have you noticed that the same things you have done many times over (kissing, caressing, even making love) can have vastly different qualities depending on your approach and your state of mind? Have you noticed how much control you have over those variables? Have you found that when the focus is decidedly on intimacy that there is no ceiling placed on pleasure or passion? Have you noticed a stronger spiritual connection as part of your stronger Living Room and Bedroom connection?

As you move into the final steps in the *CoupleFlow* Program, we encourage you to continue nurturing the Bedroom of your relationship in multiple ways. Get beyond your old routines. Keep making time to enjoy each other and to keep things fresh and fun. Keep reinforcing everything you know that works for you and everything that keeps you in your *CoupleFlow* and enjoying Sexual Abundance.

Putting It All Together

Why This Matters:

This PIE is the next natural step in your progression of sensual and erotic PIEs. You now have an opportunity to draw from the broader menu of sensual pleasures you have developed with each other, and to add another item. This item itself may be familiar to each of you, but after cultivating the renewed connection that you have, you may notice that it has a novel quality. Though this PIE includes having intercourse, you are encouraged to maintain the perspective that rather than the *main course*, this is merely the *next course*. Even if you have been together or married for many years, this is a time to celebrate your privilege to be able to enjoy each other in this incredibly special way.

Guidelines:

- First, enjoy a relaxing bath or shower together, then take turns caressing each other's bodies.
- Enjoy some *Post-Game Entertainment* as you kiss passionately.
- After you have enjoyed each other's bodies, move into position for intercourse, pausing to enjoy genital to genital stimulation without entry, perhaps using a personal lubricant to enhance your comfort and pleasure.
- After enjoying the external genital to genital pleasuring, move toward intercourse. As you pursue your own pleasure, continuing communicating about your comfort and preferences, redirecting each other as needed.
- Gaze into each other's eyes to enhance your connection.

- Try positions that you both find fun and exciting, following your arousal wherever it leads you.
- After you have concluded your intercourse time, maintain your presence with each other, noticing the sensations in your body as well as your emotions.

Talk about it:

- What did you enjoy the most? Did you encounter any barriers?
- What felt different/similar compared to your previous intercourse experiences with each other?
- What might you want to try the next time? A different position? More or different foreplay?
- What feelings were you aware of, and what are you feeling toward your partner now?

*Rate it:*_____

BEDROOM FUN FOR EVERYONE!

The *CoupleFlow* program provides multiple opportunities to reevaluate your Bedroom experience. If you notice a tendency toward your old intercourse patterns, you can jointly consider which of them to keep in the mix, which ones you'd like to discard and any new ideas you might want to try. For example, take the couple that for years has had a predictable pattern of:

kissing →

    genital stimulation →

        her orgasm →

            entry →

                his orgasm →

                    done

They may want to experiment with a longer period of kissing, or to try a vibrator or other toy that might be fun, or try a room other than the Bedroom, or to try a time of day that they wouldn't normally try, or to be in total darkness, or to linger longer after intercourse, or try some role playing, or....

Obviously, there are endless possibilities when you have engineered your *CoupleFlow* to lead you toward Sexual Abundance. You will keep moving into these possibilities together in a way that feels natural, fun and exciting. By now you have a vastly expanded menu of pleasurable activities. The following two PIEs can be fun activities in and of themselves or they can lead to more. That's up to you to decide, but the main point is to make sure your Bedroom is a FUN-room.

Trail of Kisses

> *"I could spend hours getting lost in her body."*
> *-Nick, 44*

Why This Matters:

This PIE gives you another great option for increasing Bedroom fun and eroticism. It can be a great way to get out of a rut and to reconnect with the energy that may have been more naturally present in the earlier stages of your relationship. So even if you have limited experience with trails in the great outdoors, there's nothing to stop you from blazing new trails in the Bedroom.

Guidelines:

- After bathing or showering together, make your Bedroom as dark as possible and get into bed together nude.
- The first receiver will find a comfortable position lying face down on the bed.
- As the caresser, you will begin making a trail of kisses from your partner's face and head down to his/her feet.
- As the receiver, you can turn over and allow the caresser to make a new trail of kisses on the front side of your body.
- As the caresser, feel free to linger *anywhere* along the way. When you have each thoroughly enjoyed this most pleasurable trail-blazing, switch roles to allow for equal opportunity. There is no pre-determined ending to this PIE -- just trust that you will take the trail wherever it is supposed to lead you.

Talk about it:

- What were your favorite trails as the trail blazer? As the receiver?
- Are you aware of anything that might have helped your experience be better?
- What feelings were you aware of? How are you feeling toward your partner now?

Rate it:_____

Shall We Dance?

> *"I've always loved the electricity between us when we dance."*
> *-Tanya, 54*

Why This Matters:

This activity combines passion, fun and eroticism with music and dancing. If you do not consider yourself a good dancer, don't worry -- no real skill is required, just an openness to letting loose a little bit! This PIE can be a great reflection of how you are moving into Sexual Abundance. This isn't because you've been hanging from the chandelier (unless you have), but because you've been very intentional about nurturing both the Living Room and the Bedroom of your relationship.

In the Bedroom, you've been cultivating presence by slowing things down. This has allowed for a heightened awareness of what you are experiencing together. In the Living Room, you've been making conscious contributions to your *CoupleFlow* (through direct and respectful communication, by looking for opportunities to share joy, affirmation and gratitude, etc.). Through it all, you've been having fun while growing closer. This PIE is set up to continue that trend. Let the music play!

Guidelines:

- You will need a device (iPod, CD Player, etc.) that can play your favorite songs. Each of you will come prepared with at least two songs that you would like to dance to with your partner. You can choose from a full range of genres and tempos, the only criteria being that you think it would be a fun song for this PIE.

- After bathing or showering (optional), get back into some light, comfortable clothing. Then, decide who will play the first song (alternate choice after each song ends).

Song 1: Dance to this song with your clothes on.

Song 2: As the music begins this time, *each of you will remove the other's outer clothes, leaving only your underwear on for this dance.*

Song 3: As the music begins to play this time, *you will remove each other's underwear so you can dance naked to this song.*

Song 4: You might want to keep dancing to song number four, or you might wish to get into bed and enjoy each other there as the music plays on. There is no predetermined end point for this PIE. If it leads to sexual touching or intercourse, great! If not, then at least you have created a hot, new dance club right in your own home!

Talk about it:

- What did you enjoy the most?
- Did you encounter any barriers?
- What feelings were you aware of? What are you feeling toward your partner right now?

Rate it:_____

Was it Spiritual for *You*?

*"There are times when everything is
so intensely wonderful that I feel
transported to another realm."*
-Ashley, 39

Why This Matters:

As you come down the *CoupleFlow* homestretch, one of the
differences you may be aware of is the enhanced connection you
feel with each other, inside and outside the Bedroom. As you look
back on the many experiences you have shared with each other
during this process, one or more may stand out for you as
especially meaningful moments of connection. You might even go
so far as to place moments like these in the "spiritual" category. It
might not be the first time you have ever felt this way in your
partner's presence, but by now you may have a better idea about
the conditions that need to be present in order to achieve this level
of connection.

You know that having a spiritual connection with your partner is
not happenstance. It is a natural destination arrived at when you
are so gratefully connected with your in-the-moment experience
that you seem to transcend your typical state of mind and enter into
a wonderfully altered state. You have not lost touch with reality
during those moments, but in fact are as closely connected with it
as you could ever be. When these moments occur through a shared
activity with your partner, a special layer of bonding is added to
the fabric of your relationship. The authenticity and vulnerability
of these shared moments are often characterized by very powerful
emotions and sensations (gratitude, joy, love, passion, pleasure,
etc). By reflecting on these moments personally and then sharing
them with your partner, you not only reinforce the strong bond

between you, but also you give rise to the hope that you can continue to nurture your spiritual connection in the future.

Guidelines:

Reflect on a time during this program when you experienced a spiritual moment (Bedroom or Living Room) in your partner's presence, and write about it as it unfolded chronologically. As you write this narrative, be mindful of the following:

- Was there any *relevant context* for this moment? (the first time you had taken a bath together in years; a recent loss; a recent accomplishment)
- Was there anything about the conditions that made things feel more special than usual?
- What was actually *happening* at the time?
- What *emotional feelings* were you aware of?
- What *bodily sensations* were you aware of?
- Why does this moment stand out?
- What made it feel spiritual?

Share your spiritual moments with each other and discuss your reactions to hearing each other's narrative.

Gratitude Letter

> *Her commitment to me and our relationship has never been more obvious and I have never been more thankful for it."*
> *-Derrick, 51*

Why This Matters:

Gratitude is one feeling that is universally experienced when living in abundance. It is likely that you have a vastly enhanced awareness of gratitude for many things resulting from your experiences in this program. Because you have been working so closely with each other, you likely have much gratitude not only for what you have *achieved* but also what you have *appreciated* about each other's efforts. Now is a great time to connect with those feelings and to share them with each other.

One of the most powerful ways to increase intimacy is to express your gratitude directly to your partner. When we *experience* gratitude, we open ourselves to move in the direction of the person for whom we feel grateful. This requires some vulnerability. When we actually *express* gratitude, we embrace an additional layer of vulnerability. And when we *focus* on gratitude, like anything else we focus on, it *expands*. The positive flow of intimacy and abundance between your Living Room and Bedroom are accelerated and deepened by the focus on and expression of gratitude for everything you have with each other.

Guidelines:

Part I: Make a list of as many things that you can think of that you appreciate regarding your partner's contributions during this program. You may find the following questions helpful in organizing your thoughts.

- When were you aware that your partner was doing something that did not come naturally and therefore required some additional thought or focus or courage?
- When do you recall your partner being sensitive or aware of your feelings during a difficult time for you?
- When were you aware of your partner following through on a commitment?
- When did you notice your partner making you and/or your relationship a priority?

Part II: Once you complete your list, write a letter to your partner expressing your gratitude for each item on your list. Take turns reading your letters to each other, and make a copy for your partner to keep. Finally, share your reactions to hearing each other's letter as well as what it was like to actually write your letter.

- Remember that the feelings of gratitude you connected with *during* this PIE were there *before* this PIE, just waiting to be discovered, embraced, enjoyed and shared. This is a process you can engage over and over again well beyond the conclusion of this program. Every time you express gratitude, you *absolutely* enhance the connection between Living Room and Bedroom and energize your *CoupleFlow* as you go.

Couple's Gratitude Journal

> *I love looking back at the entries from a year ago and being reminded of our areas of appreciation at the time.*
> *-Meredith, 40*

Why This Matters:

Did you ever notice how easy it can be to notice the ways in which your partner doesn't always do things to your liking or seems to fall short of your hopes or expectations? There may be legitimate issues to discuss with each other in this regard, but your *Couple's Gratitude Journal* is the place for you to focus on what you *are* getting from your partner, and on your positive experiences of him/her. So this PIE is a great way to keep your focus exactly where it should be: On all of the ways you admire and appreciate each other. If you write in this journal consistently, you are sure to notice feelings of love and partnership crowding out any feelings of resentment. However, if you and your partner are absolutely not the journaling types, just try it for a week and see what you think.

Guidelines:

- Whether a simple notebook or something more decorative, what really counts is what's written inside your journal. You can each keep your own journal, or you can share one in which you each make separate entries. The latter method has the advantage of allowing each of you to see what the other is appreciating about you. These entries have a way of feeding off of each other, creating a positive feedback loop that is pretty hard to beat.
- There is no right or wrong way to make entries. Just think about something you genuinely appreciate about your partner and write it down. If you can think of something

specific and recent, that's great ("I know how tired you were last night and you still got our coffee station ready to go for the morning." "When I heard you laugh today it reminded me of how I've always been drawn to your laughter -- it's the best sound in the world."). But more general statements of appreciation can work also ("I've always admired how you go out of your way to help others.")

- If you are each keeping your own journals, choose a time to share your entries, or you can have an open-door policy so anytime either of you wants to see how you've being appreciated you can take a peek. Either way, you will be on the same, appreciative page.

What I Know Now

Why This Matters:

You know some things now about your relationship's *CoupleFlow* that you could not possibly have known before beginning this program: Everything from how to talk about things that matter to each of you in the Living Room to how to have more consistency and fun in the Bedroom. Now you have the ongoing opportunity to put them to use! This PIE allows each of you to take stock of specific areas of awareness that have been developed and/or enhanced. Being specific and concrete allows you to more clearly identify and claim the gains you have made. As you do, there is a great opportunity to experience gratitude. This PIE also serves as a stepping stone to creating your *"Lifetime Blueprint for Optimal CoupleFlow"* at the end of this chapter.

Guidelines:

Please respond to the following as completely and specifically as possible. During your scheduled PIE time you will take turns reading your responses with the option of discussing any of them in more detail. (Examples from other couples have been provided).

1. **What do you know or understand about *yourself* that is more than you knew or understood before beginning this program?**
   ("I understand how easily I end up feeling resentful when I don't ask for what I need or want." "I understand I need to work on not feeling like a child when you ask me to do something." "I understand that I tend to withhold my true

feelings- in the Living Room and Bedroom- but I'm seeing how to do things differently.")

2. **What do you know or understand about your *partner* that is more than you knew or understood before beginning this program?**

("I understand that you really love me despite all my shortcomings;" "I understand that certain things are powerful triggers for you to feel scared and that your fear often looks like anger;" "I understand how unworthy and inadequate you have always felt and how you assume I see you that way too.")

3. **What do you know or understand about your *sexual* self that is more than you knew or understood before beginning this program?**

("I never realized that I can enjoy your touch just for the pleasure it brings and not have it be merely a stepping stone to sex;" "I'm seeing how much else there is to my sexuality beyond just having sex and I'm excited to share it with you;" "I'm learning that I need to ask for what I want sexually, but I'm also realizing how *hard* it is for me to ask.")

4. **What do you know or understand about your partner's sexual self that is more than you knew or understood before beginning this program?**

("You need to feel safe before you can enjoy our times together and I'm starting to understand what that means;" "You can slow down and enjoy our shared moments instead of rushing ahead to your moment -- and it's wonderful!")

5. **What do you know about your *shared times together* (Living Room and/or Bedroom) as a result of your experiences in this program?** ("If we get the kids to bed a half hour earlier we end up with a half hour to enjoy each other" "Five minutes of connect time at the end of a crazy busy day goes a long way" "Sexual Abundance is not just a concept-- we set our minds to do things differently and now we know exactly what it is and that it's for *us*" "We learned how to put the luster back on a relationship that had lost its shine through the years.")

Finishing Instructions:

After the examples in the following space, make a list of everything you've learned or have come to appreciate through your experiences in this program. Refer back to your responses from this PIE as well as to your notes from all of the previous PIEs to jog your memory.

What I've Learned Through this Program

If we schedule time together, we're a lot more likely to actually have some fun together, AND there's still room to be spontaneous.
The Daily Shares are like working out in the gym; I don't always want to do them, but I'm always glad I did.
I really like being there for you.
I have more satisfying experiences when I pursue my own pleasure.
When I start wishing we had more fun together there are things *I* can do to help that along.
There's nothing like getting a flirty or encouraging text from you to keep me going during a long day!
The Adult's Menu is always better than the Children's Menu. And I really need to be aware of the menu item about avoidance.
Our Gratitude Journal is my favorite book.

Lifetime Blueprint for Optimal *CoupleFlow*

> *"If you don't know where you're going, you'll end up someplace else."*
> - Yogi Berra

Why This Matters:

You have been quite committed to developing your very own *CoupleFlow*. As a result, there is a noticeably energized dynamic between the Living Room and the Bedroom of your relationship. Now it is time to develop a master plan to make sure you can enjoy and build upon what you have created in an ongoing and practical way. Your *Lifetime Blueprint* will be a written record of everything you have come to value in your progress to date. It is not only a list of these values, but an *action plan*. You can be just as intentional with the plan you are about to create for yourselves as you have been with the plan we created for you.

Specifically detailing the active steps required to continue your momentum makes any short or long term goals for optimal circulation between your Living Room and Bedroom much more realistic. It also helps to insure that you will continue living in alignment with the vision you developed earlier in this program. When you see your finished Lifetime Blueprint, you can take pride in recognizing that it was your courage, trust and mutual commitments that made this document possible.

Guidelines:

Part I: Compare the lists each of you made at the end of your *"What I Know Now"* PIE. Notice items that are similar and any items that appear only on one of your lists. Once you have compared your lists, *merge them into one Master List*, using the upcoming template titled "Our Master List." Rank the items in order with the most important items near the top. The general rule is, "If it is important to *one* of us, it should be on our Master List." Some negotiation may be required. For example, let's say your partner's list includes, "Scheduling time to enjoy each other," and yours does not. Then it would be helpful to reach a compromise regarding where scheduling could fit on your Master List.

Part II: For each item on the Master List, you will write a corresponding action statement. For example, if "scheduling time to enjoy each other," makes it onto your Master List, an appropriate action statement would be, "We will meet each Sunday after putting the kids to bed to agree on at least one scheduled time during the week to enjoy some sensual/sexual intimacy" or "We will stick with our Thursday 'nooner' because it's been working great!"

The series of clear action statements, taken together, become a blueprint for you to follow for at least the short-term and possibly for the rest of your lives. Like any good plan, it is designed to produce desired outcomes when followed consistently, yet flexible enough to be adjusted from time to time. Above all else, it is *uniquely yours*. Your experiences during this program were *yours*, the values and insights that grew out of those experiences are *yours* and the action steps in your Lifetime Blueprint are *yours*. It might be helpful to refer to the upcoming sample as you convert your Master List into the Lifetime Blueprint itself.

Lifetime Blueprint for Optimal *CoupleFlow*

(Sample)

1. We will plan our PIE times for the week Sundays at 8PM.
2. We will meet for Daily Shares every night at 8:30 (except Wednesday night--9PM) and we'll alternate responsibility for initiating on weekly basis.
3. We will reserve one or two PIEs/week for pleasuring that leads to intercourse and one PIE that does not. (PIEs can come from this book or we can make our own PIEs!)
4. We will define successful experiences by how present and connected we feel (not by how intense the experience is).
5. We will kiss passionately on a regular basis, just to enjoy kissing (not only during our sexual times).
6. We commit to practicing the *Adult to Adult Communicating* PIE as a general rule, but especially when we feel uncomfortable or anxious about discussing something. This works for us!
7. We are each responsible for our own pleasure: We will welcome redirection in keeping with this approach.
8. We will send at least one flirty text to each other/week.
9. We will revisit the fantasies we shared with each other and add to them as we go forward.
10. We will take one entire day (or weekend)/quarter for our relationship (B&B; camping; hotel on the beach).
11. We will review this Lifetime Blueprint at our 1st Daily Share of the month and ask: "How are we doing?"
12. We will meet with our therapist on a quarterly basis to review and revise our *Lifetime Blueprint*.

Our Master List

A View from the Top

> *"We take our fate out of the hands of chance by consciously realizing the conditions that we desire to see manifested in our lives."*
> *- The Master Key System*

Why This Matters:

Picking up where Step Four left off, this PIE is designed to capture each of your visions for your thriving relationship. This is your relationship at full-power as a result of the *CoupleFlow* you will only continue to strengthen and enjoy. The vision you connect with in this PIE is a key component of increasing your intimacy potential: You first need to see clearly how your relationship looks in its ideal (but still realistic) form in order to keep things headed in that direction. As you continue to refine your vision, you keep raising the ceiling on your intimacy potential. In addition to clarifying your own vision, this PIE also gives you a window into how your partner imagines the best version of your relationship.

Guidelines:

You may want to review your responses from: 1. The *"Future"* portions of the *"Past, Present and Future"* PIE 2. The *"Hello"* and *"Keep"* lists from the *"Hello & Goodbye"* PIE and 3. Your responses from the *"Our Legacy"* PIE. Next, imagine that you are enjoying a wonderful era in your relationship. You might see some areas of sadness or chronic frustration that have been transformed, both in the Living Room and the Bedroom. You clearly see the version of yourself that you really like, as you are able to be true to yourself in this relationship. You see how you are freely and fully enjoying sexual intimacy and all of its abundant possibilities. You see yourself experiencing more and more pleasure, comfort, presence, fun and joy with your partner.

Allow yourself to see all of this and to feel whatever is there, especially focusing on gratitude, joy and serenity. When you have a clear connection with your image of this and a good connection with the accompanying feelings, write a narrative about it. Do not be concerned with how lengthy it is, but do try to be as detailed as possible. As you describe what you see from this "mountaintop," consider the following to guide you.

- How do you feel about yourself in this relationship? (confident, content, loveable?)

- What is different about what you see in this relationship?

- What dysfunctional or even destructive behaviors are absent?

- What have you chosen to retain from your past/present in this relationship?

- What does your facial expression and body language look like? What about your partner's?

- What kinds of activities do you see yourselves doing?

- What feelings do you notice as you envision this relationship?

When you have finished writing your narrative, share your "View from the Top" with your partner.

Marry Me Again[18]

> *"To hear how deeply he loves me and specifically how he appreciates me and how committed he is to us... I have no words to describe how much that meant."*
> —Margarita, 43

Why This Matters:

Much has likely changed since the time you originally committed to each other. If you've been together long enough, you may see yourself and your partner as different people today, at least in some respects. To make it this far, you have necessarily persevered through many relationship rough spots, and your anniversary number has climbed. As the years go by, do you ever wonder if your partner would choose you today, knowing everything s/he knows about you that s/he didn't know way back when? Do you ever wish you could let your partner know that you absolutely *would* do it all over again? Here's your chance to do just that, by writing vows that honor your history and represent your current values and promises.

Guidelines:

Step One. Reflect on what drew you to your partner when your relationship was just getting off the ground.

---

[18] This PIE is just as important for couples who are not legally married, either by choice or lack of legal option to do so, as it is for married couples. Vows are promises, and promises matter whether recognized by the state or not.

Step Two. Reflect on what you have grown to appreciate in new ways about your partner. These are characteristics or qualities that you may not have been aware of until later in your relationship.

Step Three. Reflect on some of the challenges you have faced together and how they have made you stronger as a couple.

Step Four. Reflect on what your partner means to you, and what you want your partner to know beyond any doubt regarding his/her place in your life.

Step Five. Reflect on your responses above to arrive at what you would like to promise to your partner. These items may be similar in many ways to your original vows, but should represent your up to the minute commitments.

*****

Now write a brief letter to your partner, using steps 1-4 as your introduction to your new vows in step five. Discuss with your partner how you would like to share your new vows with each other and how you would like to mark the occasion. Would you like your children or any other witnesses present? Would you like to get dressed up for a fancy dinner or perhaps throw a party of some kind? How about a Couple's Weekend away? Or perhaps something more casual in front of the fireplace after the kids have gone to bed? It's up to you!

Chapter Seven

How Good Can This Get?

Dear Readers,

Because we began this book with a letter, we thought it appropriate to sign-off with one as well. If you are reading this chapter, you have accomplished a great deal in reaching the finish line of this program, so please let us offer you our most sincere and heartfelt congratulations! Like most great accomplishments in life, it is only achieved with a clear vision for a better way and unwavering dedication to a plan of action. We envisioned this landing place when we developed the *CoupleFlow* model, and in reaching the conclusion of this program, you have established a new framework for a *lifetime* of well-founded hopefulness. It is so hopeful because it is grounded in the consistently positive and bonding interactions you have with each other, in the Living Room and the Bedroom.

In the beginning of this book, you were told that no matter where you were starting from, a moderate investment of time and energy in this program could elevate your coupleship to newfound heights. We told you that we knew how busy you were and that we had a plan for you that was as efficient as it was powerful. We told you that a more passionate, energized connection was there for you if you were willing to take charge of the feedback loop between the Living Room and the Bedroom of your relationship. We asked you to understand that the *CoupleFlow* model was *built for lasting improvements*, and that any temperature climb in the Bedroom would need to grow out of a warm and welcome Living Room. You took a leap of faith and dove in.

You might have started out with high hopes, and now you see how well-founded those hopes were. Because of your combined efforts, you now know yourselves and each other better than ever before. You feel more comfortable sharing your realities with

> *We told you that a more passionate, energized connection was there for you if you were willing to take charge of the feedback loop between the Living Room and the Bedroom of your relationship.*

each other honestly and respectfully. You have become more skilled in moving toward each other without sacrificing your individuality. Your emotional intimacy is noticeably improved because there is a much more secure attachment bond between you than ever existed before. But life is still challenging, and sometimes you fail to treat each other as the partners you truly are. That bond is preserved and even strengthened

The process of sharing yourselves in this way has followed you right into your Bedroom, where you now enjoy a greater sense of freedom, presence, joy and fun. You realize how your sexuality has evolved during this process and how the sexual intimacy you share has been enhanced. By strategically slowing things down, your menu of pleasurable activities has been expanded, and your passion has followed. Instead of asking, "Why don't we do this more often?" you actually *ARE* doing "this" more often. You are

> *Instead of asking, "Why don't we do this more often?" you actually ARE doing "this" more often.*

enjoying the energizing power of your optimized *CoupleFlow* and are connecting with the essence of *Sexual Abundance*: a renewable system of intimacy and pleasure that seems to just keep getting better. And just to reinforce your progress, take a minute to revisit that little relationship quiz from earlier in this book. We've reprinted it on the following page and we know you'll see measurable improvements.

_____ Frequency of Bedroom activities

_____ Initiation (who approaches whom)

_____ Sexual satisfaction   (arousal/orgasm/fun)

_____ Variety (activities/settings /positions)

_____ Sexual communication

1 = This is a significant concern.

2- = A lot of room for improvement

3 = It's OK, but could be even better.

4 = I feel good about this part of our sex life.

5- I wouldn't change a thing!

These positive trends are not due to coincidence but to your own actions. You are *intentionally nurturing* the sexual intimacy in your relationship and allowing yourself to be nurtured by it. When you see the results of your actions, you can trust the progress you have made, knowing that *you* have the power to continue being proactive.

As you look back on your experiences in this program, you can see how your sexual times together have become more playful, fun and experimental. Furthermore, your relationship is characterized by trust, partnership, respect and appreciation more than ever before. You also probably noticed your spirituality (however you define it) growing stronger and providing another source of bonding.

No matter where you started from, you have worked diligently to make this wonderfully transformative shift. As a result, you are aware of what you now have in place and of what great potential the future holds. What a strong position to hold, where you can *continue* to reap the benefits of the work you have done.

Nevertheless, you should allow for those times or cycles when one of you is less available or less relational than you would prefer. The fact is, life will remain challenging no matter how strong your *CoupleFlow* is, and sometimes you will fail to treat each other as the partners you truly are.

> *You understand that your greatest victories as a couple are not defined by the absence of difficulties, but by your partnership in response to them.*

These occasional lapses back into old ways of thinking, feeling and behaving that cause ruptures now represent opportunities to grow closer because you know how to repair from them. Your repair skills and your resilience allow you to pull yourselves back into partnership. These occasional slips feel different than before because you can talk about them safely, averting blame and short-circuiting resentment. You understand that your greatest victories as a couple are not defined by the absence of difficulties, but by your partnership in response to them.

We might take certain things for granted in life, but no matter how well things are flowing, we *cannot rest on our relationship laurels.* That is why you developed your *Lifetime Blueprint.* It represents

> *No matter how well things are flowing, we cannot rest on our relationship laurels.*

the most important concepts you have learned and the best practices you have developed. What happens from here on out is fairly predictable: If you consistently review and follow your Blueprint, you will consistently optimize your *CoupleFlow* and experience Sexual Abundance on an ever deepening level. You'll feel the energy in your Living Room and Bedroom feeding into one another, creating the kind of atmosphere where you both feel consistently appreciated and desired. And the best news of all? *There is no ceiling* on all of that connecting energy. *You get to decide* to keep nurturing this system -- *your system* -- that rewards you in infinitely abundant ways, and is ready to repair as needed.

So, it is all there for you now: Your, intimacy-based, self-reinforcing system that you can enjoy and continue developing for the rest of your lives together. Your dedicated commitment keeps the sun rising in your hearts, shining brightly on the precious jewel that is your relationship. Now, with your strengthened *CoupleFlow*, you may very well find yourselves wondering,

"How GOOD can this get?"

May this question occur to you often and may you always find the answer in each other's love.

Warmest regards always,

Bill & Ginger

Bibliography

Bader, Michael. (2003). *Arousal: The secret logic of sexual fantasies.* New York, NY: St. Martin's Griffin.

Bercaw, B & G. (2010). *The couple's guide to intimacy: how sexual reintegration therapy can help your relationship heal.* Pasadena, CA: CCH.

Brown, C. B. (2012). *Daring greatly : how the courage to be vulnerable transforms the way we live, love, parent, and lead* (1st ed.). New York, NY: Gotham Books.

Carnes, P., & Schwartz, B. K. (2010). *Facing the shadow : starting sexual and relationship recovery : a gentle path to beginning recovery from sex addiction* (2nd ed.). Carefree, Ariz.: Gentle Path Press.

Gary, W. (2013). Your Brain on Porn. from http://www.yourbrainonporn.com

Haanel, Charles F. (2008). The new master key system. Hillsboro, OR: Atria Books/Beyond Words.

Hendrix, H. (2008). *Getting the love you want : a guide for couples* (20th anniversary ed.). New York: H. Holt And Co.

Jackson, S. A., & Csikszentmihalyi, M. (1999). *Flow in sports.* Champaign, IL: Human Kinetics.

Katehakis, A. (2010). *Erotic intelligence: Igniting hot, healthy sex while in recovery from sex addiction.* Deerfield Beach, FL: Health Communications, Inc.

Lancer, H. (2014). *Younger: The breakthrough anti-anging method for radiant skin.* New York, NY: Grand Central Life & Style.

McCarthy, B. & McCarthy, Emily. (2003). *"Rekindling desire: a step-by-step program for low-sex and no-sex marriages.* New York, NY: Brunner-Routledge.

Mellody, P., Miller, A. W., & Miller, K. (1989). *Facing codependence : what it is, where it comes from, how it sabotages our lives* (1st ed.). San Francisco: Perennial Library.

Mellody, P., Miller, A. W., & Miller, K. (1992). *Facing love addiction : giving yourself the power to change the way you love : the love connection to codependence* (1st ed.). New York, NY: HarperSan Francisco.

Satir, V. (2014). PAIRS. from http://www.pairs.com/dtr.php

Siegel, D. J. (2010). *Mindsight : the new science of personal transformation* (1st ed.). New York: Bantam Books.

Siegel, D. & Bryson, T.P. (2011). *The whole brain child: 12 revolutionary strategies to nurture your child's developing mind.* New York: Bantam Books.

SRI. (2014). Sexual Recovery Institute. from http://www.sexualrecovery.com

Acknowledgements

This book has been the result of many years of input and guidance from a wonderful array of people we are fortunate to call family friends and esteemed colleagues (and many of you fall into more than one of these categories!). Bill's mother, **Kathleen Rose Bercaw**, a distinguished retired columnist and feature writer, spent countless hours with various iterations of manuscripts. Her style and copy edits significantly elevated the book's all-around quality. Her emotional support during the writing and publishing process was every bit as valuable. Thanks, Mom! And also thank you to Bill's father, **Bill**, for his unwavering faith in us and his consistent encouragement. We also thank Ginger's parents, **Terry and Jayann Flood,** for the many times they have traveled to stay with our children, allowing us to attend professional conferences or writing weekends. This has allowed us many valuable opportunities to focus on the book jointly. Thanks for all you've done! We are also fortunate to have a small army of fierce proponents in our families, including **Anthony and Shan Bercaw, Jon and Elaine Patti**; **Noelle Mineweaser**; **Terace Patti; Bob and Juanita Conn**, and **Doris Flood**. And we could not be happier with superstar, **Rob Weiss**, for writing such a heartfelt Foreword and to **Alex Katehakis** for her enthusiastic endorsement. Rob and Alex, we hope to follow your leads in spreading healthy relationships around the globe and to doing your profession proud.

One of the smartest things we did during the writing process was to run two focus groups. We received such valuable input from the many friends who volunteered to read a draft of the book and to share their reactions to a long list of questions. And when it came to finding a moderator for these groups, only the best would do, so we invited **John Clark** to do the honors. Thanks also to John's wife, **Karen**, not only for her participation but for lending him to us for several focus groups and strategy dinners.

Amber Franklin went above and beyond in her reading and re-reading of the book. We were touched by her obvious investment in the quality of this book and in us. Her feedback was consistently spot-on (and we dared not cross her!) Another La Canada All-Star, **Anne Goodwin**, came up big for us, copy and style editing the entire book. We don't know how she found time to do all that with the schedule she keeps, but we sure do appreciate it (any typos appearing in the book could only have occurred post-Annie's edits!) We also have deep appreciation for all the ladies who participated in the focus groups (some more than once): **Carrie Walker, Ann Pearson, Maren Pellant, Karen Clarke, Anne Goodwin, Jackie Chuang, Amber Franklin, Lulu Cates, Frannie Jett, Julie Lin, Una Battaglia, Tracy Smith, Nicolette Fuerst and Claire Hart.** We also thank **Rene Pak** for all the work she did in helping us to organize these focus groups and on various other book-related tasks.

Brandy Allport set a world record for high-quality, copy edit turn-around time. **Tina Bryson's** consultation around interpersonal neurobiology was extremely helpful, as was her author-to-author encouragement. **Joel Newton** (yes, the Oscar-nominated, Golden Globe winning filmmaker) dedicated the better part of the same weekend he was hosting a Super Bowl party for his beloved Seahawks to making our crowdfunding video. We ended up with a great video and Joel ended up with a blowout victory, so it all worked out! Thanks for lending him, **Cathy**!

Good friends are like gold and we thank the **Battaglia, Lin, Pearson, Asghari and Hart** families for many years of laughter, confidence and always being there. **Julie, Una, Claire, Homeira and Ann**, you are so special.

To **Shelly Lennox**, a true angel of a caregiver to our children, our deepest thanks for being such a ray of light in their lives and for becoming a valued member of our family. To our amazing assistant, **Piper Grant** and her fiancé (the book's cover designer), **Sergio Saucedo**, we are so lucky to have you on our side! To **Kim Hruba**, (*Elevator Girl* author) thank you for taking the time to walk us through the crowdfunding process and for style editing our book cover. We can't wait to see *Elevator Girl* take off! To **Dr. Barbara Levinson**, we are so appreciative of your encouragement through the years and for your extremely helpful review of our book. We always look so forward to seeing you! We also thank **Dr. Jan Beauregard** for taking the time to so thoroughly read our book and provide such thoughtful feedback. We also greatly appreciate **Staci Sprout's** input and affirmation.

To **Michele Canon** and the wonderful folks at **Foothill Family Services**, thanks so much for partnering with us and we look forward to supporting the tremendous work you all do. To **Anthony Mattero**, (Foundry Literary + Media) for believing in this book and for guiding us in the proposal writing process. We have a feeling we still may do something great together down the line! (despite your Orange roots)

We thank our teachers and mentors, including **Dr. Herbert Potash** and **Dr. John Duryee**, **Dr. Ed Shafranske**, **Dr. Robert deMayo**, **Dr. Clifford and Joyce Penner**, **Dr. Patrick Carnes**, and **Pia Mellody** for exposing us to treatment models and ways of life that inspired and strengthened us. To our publicists, **Caroline Tanaka, Jeanne Beach and Melissa Penn**, we thank you for getting us and our book out there! To Pubslush's **Sara Mendelson**, thank you for guiding us through a process with which we were so unfamiliar.

Bill thanks **Brett Franklin and Steve Battaglia** for lending humorous perspective to the book (though thankfully for our readers none of it actually appeared in these pages).

*****

In the spirit of saving the *best for last,* we must thank our amazing children. **Elizabeth and Jamie** have been hearing about this book for the past 5 years, and sometimes have not had as much of us as we all would have preferred due to our writing responsibilities. You two have been so patient and so supportive and we hope that you will always follow your dreams like we are following ours. And as for what you're probably most interested in, all we can say is, *"We're going to Disneyland!"*

Made in the USA
San Bernardino, CA
16 March 2014